THE
BIOGRAPH

OR, A HISTORIC ___UN C.

THE DEVIL AND HIS FIERY DOMINIONS

DISCLOSING THE ORIENTAL ORIGIN OF THE BELIEF IN A
DEVIL AND FUTURE ENDLESS PUNISHMENT; ALSO, AN
EXPLANATION OF THE PAGAN ORIGIN OF THE
SCRIPTURAL TERMS, BOTTOMLESS PIT, LAKE OF
FIRE AND BRIMSTONE, CHAINS OF DARK-
NESS, CASTING OUT DEVILS. WORM
THAT NEVER DIETH, ETC.

By KERSEY GRAVES

Author of " The World's Sixteen Crucified Saviors"

WITH FORWARDS

by PAUL TICE
Author of "Triumph of the Human Spirit:
The Greatest Achievements of the Human Soul
and How Its Power can Change Your Life"

and MARSHALL J. GAUVIN
Author of "Fundamentals of Freethought"

THE BOOK TREE
Escondido, California

Fifth Edition

Republished from the fourth edition, 1924

Biography of Satan
ISBN 1-885395-11-6

Published by
The Book Tree
Post Office Box 724
Escondido, CA 92033

Call (800) 700-TREE for a FREE BOOK TREE CATALOG
with over 1000 Books, Booklets, Audio, and Video on
Alchemy, Ancient Mysteries, Anti-Gravity, Atlantis, Free
Energy, Gnosticism, Health Issues, Magic, Metaphysics,
Mythology, Occult, Rare Books, Religious Controversy,
Sitchin Studies, Spirituality, Symbolism, Tesla, and much
more. Or visit our website at www.thebooktree.com

Forward to Fifth Edition

Does the Devil exist? If so, where is he? Is he in that fiery place called hell? Or is he just a figment of man's imagination? We've been asking these questions for centuries and although many claim to know the answers, no one has ever come forward with convincing proof of any kind, pro or con, to the existence of Satan. That is, until now.

What we mean by "convincing proof" is solid historical evidence – knowing and examining the context of the Satan stories and the true meanings of words used in them. This is by far the best avenue of approach (which Kersey Graves takes), rather than pointing to any terrible historic event, like the Nagasaki nuclear explosion, and saying, "It must have been the Devil." There is no real proof with that or anything similar – it just shows that something terrible happened.

This book goes straight to the root of the stories, Biblical and otherwise, to expose the origins of the Devil. You may not like what you read, but after reading it it becomes difficult, in many places, to argue against Graves' thesis. And that thesis is that the Devil is nothing more than a fabricated "bad guy" created by the early Christian priesthood to keep the people in line.

If this sounds absurd or unlikely, keep reading. Increasing numbers of people, especially scholars, are coming to realize that much of the Bible is *not* literal. In other words, it did not happen. It is a story. As Jesus taught in parables, so did the Bible.

Some powerful and spiritual things could well have happened in Biblical times, that is clear, but it is equally clear that much in the Bible was also embellished or outright fabricated in order to serve the aims of the controlling priesthood. Kersey Graves claims, in this important work, that the entire character of Satan falls into this category. For many, this may be hard to accept, but the reasoning and evidence put forth in this volume can not, and should not, be taken lightly. It is a well-researched piece of work, worth the attention of every thinking person, religious and non-religious alike.

Whether you agree with him or not is not so important. What really matters is that you may begin to see a bigger picture. You may start *questioning* issues like this one – the existence of the Devil – for yourself, instead of accepting his existence blindly. It has been ingrained in us not to ask questions, but to simply accept what we are told.

Some, however, *do* ask questions. They want to know. They want to be more than blind believers, they want to get as close to the truth as they can during their lifetimes. I am one of those people, and maybe you are too. My questioning has led me to believe that in order to be successful in this search for truth, you must be willing to question everything. You must be willing to think for yourself, to explore areas that are sometimes off-limits to traditional beliefs, and to weed out what does not apply.

As we move forward and evolve, spiritually, we may one day discover that Kersey Graves was right. We may find that there never was a Satan or Devil – that he was just another in a long line of superstitious beliefs held by man. We will never know the truth about this or anything else until we begin to question it.

Rev. Paul Tice

FOREWORD.

By MARSHALL J. GAUVIN

Thought has a history. The intellectual life of the present is the heritage of the beliefs and doubts, the hopes and fears, of the past. We think over again the thoughts of our fathers, with such variations only as are due to broader culture. And this broader culture is the product of intellectual variations.

Thought varies in the direction of growth. But the change of thought is, for the most part, a slow process. Beliefs are tenacious, and no beliefs are more tenacious than religious beliefs.

This is because religion has to do with gods and devils; because it presumes to tell man of his place in and relation to the world and the whence and whither of his being; because it teaches the necessity of holding certain beliefs regarding these things, and because it appeals fundamentally to man's emotions—to his hope for happiness and fear of pain in another world.

These features of religious belief give religion a universal interest. All men are interested in religion. They are interested in it because it has so largely dominated the life of humanity; because for countless ages mankind lived and thought and suffered almost wholly within the confines of religious sanctions; because every step the race has taken in the direction of intellectual progress has been taken in defiance of religious authority; because the whole range of the scientific culture of our time regarding man and the universe is a challenge to, and is challenged by, the religious notions that have come down to us from the distant past.

Accordingly, the Christian and the Deist, the Theosophist and the Spiritualist, the Agnostic and the Atheist, are equally interested, though from different points of view, in the story of humanity's religious beliefs—the history of the world's religious thought.

Without a knowledge of man's past, his present cannot be understood. Yesterday's beliefs are keys to the doors of to-day's thoughts. From what yesterday's religion was, the religion of to-day has become, and on the foundations we lay down, whether flimsy or secure, the superstructure of tomorrow's thought will rise to challenge the winds of change and to be tested by the stressful storms of science.

At the bottom of the religion of the Christian world has even been and is, the belief in an eternal fiery hell, presided over by a devil, the prince of fiends. The church has ever taught and still teaches that the faithful, the devout—at best but a mere few—will be chosen to share the eternal glory of God's presence in heaven, and that the countless billions of unregenerate and unredeemed will be tortured forever in the flames of hell, under the everlasting surveillance of the Devil's malicious leer.

That atrocious doctrine—the doctrine of eternal punishment for unbelievers—has been, in every age, the mainspring, the driving force of Christianity. Armed with that belief, the church launched herself upon the Roman Empire, destroyed the pagan religions, extinguished pagan culture, overthrew classical civilization, and ushered the world into the noisome gulf of the Dark Ages.

Fired with that belief, the church filled the world with religious hate, with fanaticism, with intolerance of science and reason. Urged to desperation by that belief, the church established the Inquisition; filled the Christian world with spies and informers; and for a long succession of generations, imprisoned and stretched on racks and burnt alive, the noblest, the most progressive men and women of our race, because they had brains enough to think and courage enough to express their thought.

To satisfy that infamous belief, Hypatia and Huss, Bruno and Vanini, Servetus and Ferrer, with innumerable martyrs filling the way between the Greek teacher in the fifth century and the Spanish educator in our own day, sealed their convictions with their blood and gave their ashes to the winds.

The belief in eternal punishment gave the world a thousand religious wars. It put a ban on investigation. It gagged honest thought. It made ignorance universal and progress impossible. It put the world beneath the feet of priests. For more than fifteen hundred years, the insane notion that a hell of flames awaits the souls of unbelievers in another world did more than any other single thing to transform this world into a kind of hell.

Thundered from millions of pulpits, over and over again, during all the centuries of Christianity, that heartless belief filled the lives of men and women and children with an awful fear— a fear frequently amounting to terror—a withering fear that only recently began to pass away.

Think, for example, of these terrible words, from the lips of so otherwise good a man as the Rev. Charles H. Spurgeon, the eminent Baptist preacher of the London Metropolitan Tabernacle, only a generation ago:

"Only conceive the poor wretch in flames! See how his tongue hangs between his blistered lips! How it excoriates and burns the roof of his mouth, as though it were a firebrand! Be-

hold him crying for a drop of water! I will not
picture the scene. Suffice it for me to say that
the hell of hells will be to thee, dear sinner, the
thought that it is to be forever. Thou shalt look
up there on the throne of God   and   it thou
shalt see written: 'Forever.'

Then, dropping into v   eloquent
preacher continues:

> "Forever is written on their racks,
> Forever on their chains,
> Forever burneth in the fire;
> Forever ever reigns."

Against such frightful teachings reason has
had to fight; science has had to struggle, and the
spirit of humanity has made way but slowly. The
emancipation of the human mind is, as yet, far
from complete. The old thraldom still maintains
an ominous dominion. The chains of fear still
bind the beliefs of scores of millions. Wherever
priests and preachers are powerful, wherever the
light of modern knowledge has not yet penetrated
the dark recesses of superstition, the belief in
hell retains its hold upon the people. The whole
world of Christian orthodoxy still respects the
Devil with its belief and still honors him with the
tribute of its fear. And the ignorance and des-
potism, the confusion and war, that still darken
the face of civilization are part of the price humanity still pays for being deceived by a false

religious doctrine that has, in every Christian age, diverted man's mind from the cultivation of those concerns upon which rests his welfare in this world.

But some gains have been made. The belief in the Devil and hell has vanished from the whole intellectual world, and as education advances, the unbelievers in these terrible superstitions will multiply by the millions. The mission of education, of modern science and historical criticism, is to win the world for enlightenment, and that goal will be reached eventually, in spite of the puerile preaching of priests and the fulminations of the Fundamentalists.

But while the Devil and his fiery dominions are disappearing from the realm of man's beliefs, it must be borne in mind that belief in His Satanic Majesty and in a place of endless torment for the major portion of mankind are vital to Christianity. The reality of Satan is as plainly taught in the New Testament as is the reality of Christ. It was Satan who tempted the Son of God at the close of his forty days' fast. It was Satan who carried the younger God to the pinnacle of the Temple and thence to the top of a mountain, and offered him the kingdoms of the world, in exchange for worship.

Again and again, according to the New Testament, Christ cast devils out of human beings.

Moreover, Christ threatened men with eternal punishment in hell (Matthew xxv: 41, 46).

If these representations are not true; if the Devil is only a myth and hell but a figure of speech, the authority of the New Testament falls to the ground. With the Devil and hell gone, salvation loses its meaning; the savior is left without an office; the atonement remains unperformed; the wrath of God resolves itself into a priestly fiction—Christianity is seen to be not a divine revelation, but a gross superstition that has, for nearly two thousand years, deceived, betrayed and martyred mankind.

The author of this book has performed for his fellowmen the signal service of pointing out to them the fact that the Christian doctrine of a Devil and a hell were utterly unknown to the ancient Jews, and are nowhere taught in the Old Testament. He shows that these doctrines were derived from the mythologies of the heathen nations that surrounded the Jewish people. He shows that these doctrines were derived from the mythologies of the heathen nations that surrounded the Jewish people. He shows that the God of the Old Testament and the Devil of the New Testament—that is to say, "Our Father which art in heaven"—the God whom Christians worship—and the Lord of Hell—the God whom Christians fear—were "originally twin brothers

FOREWORD

known by the same titles," and that this God and this Devil were Chaldean sun-gods.

He shows further that the Christian notions of the "Kingdom of Heaven," of the "bottomless pit," of a "lake of fire and brimstone," and other such ideas were borrowed from Babylonian and Persian sources.

In other words, he shows that the Christian ideas as to the future worlds of bliss and torment were not made known to man by Divine revelation, but, rather, were borrowed by the founders of Christianity from the rich treasure house of pagan mythology.

Thought has a history. Christianity belongs to the natural history of thought. Its origins are found in the development and migration of mythology. And humanity is outgrowing it today because thought, illumined with knowledge, is moving to a higher plain—to the altitude of science and Rationalism.

"The Biography of Satan" is an instrument in this forward movement because it is an informing, an emancipating book, and therefore Kersey Graves, its author, was a benefactor of mankind.

Minneapolis, Minn.,
July 30. 1924.

PREFACE

In presenting the present edition of this work to the public the author deems it necessary only to add in the preface that it has been thoroughly revised and corrected, and that the numerous responses from those who availed themselves of a copy of the previous edition of the book, leaves the author no reason to doubt that the motive which actuated him in the publication of it will be fully realized. That motive was to expose and arrest the progress of the most terror-inciting superstition that ever nestled in the bosom of the ignorant, or that ever prostrated the energies of the human mind, and reduced its possessor to the condition of an abject, groveling and trembling slave!

It is common in the prefatory exegesis of a work to explain the motives which lead to its authorship or compilation. But as the motives which prompted this work are already partially disclosed in the initiatory chapter, headed "Address to the Reader," and the succeeding chapter which sets forth some of the practical evils which spring legitimately from the doctrine of future or *post mortem* punishment, we will only add to the explanation thus furnished, so far, as to state:

5

1. That notwithstanding many ages have rolled away since the after-death penalty was first originated and promulgated to the world, yet no work designed to furnish to the general reader a full, and at the same time, brief exposition of the origin and design of this mischievous doctrine, with all its various and multifarious terms, dogmas, and childish traditions, has ever before been presented to the public since an extensive inquiry has been awakened on the subject.

2. We deem it a matter of the greatest moment, that some one should make the effort to arrest the almost boundless tide of terror and misery, of which the practical dissemination of the doctrine of endless damnation has ever been and still is, a truly prolific source. For no person who has not scrutinizingly investigated the matter, can form any just or proximate conception of the extent to which the Heathen and Christian worlds have been demoralized and flooded with misery and unhappiness, by the propagation of this doctrine. These facts, wedded to the hope of checking this widespread river—this shoreless current of mischief, constitute our principal reason for publishing this work.

3. The single and serious fact, that the superstitious fear of after-death punishment furnishes the primary motive-power by which more than a million of sermons are annually dealt out from

the Christian pulpits of the United States alone,
at a cost of many millions of dollars, levied mainly
upon the pockets of the poor, which have the effect of exciting in the minds of the religious
classes the most agonizing emotions and the most
torturing fears, often producing, temporarily,
the ruin of health and happiness, even among the
most virtuous; and the people (and most of the
priests, too) being ignorant of the origin of these
alarming superstitious doctrines, the author con-
siders as ample warrant, upon moral grounds,
for attempting the task of aiding in checking the
evil and demoralizing effects of this barbarous,
anti-civilizing and terrifying heathen superstition.

Whether these reasons furnish a sufficient just-
ification for such an enterprise, is left for the can-
did reader to judge.

It is gratifying to learn that the superstitious
fear, which in every age and country in which it
has prevailed and enslaved the minds of thousands, and still holds millions in its iron grasp,
is likely to be better understood in its real nature,
its pernicious effects and in its origin.

KERSEY GRAVES

CONTENTS

CONTENTS

INTRODUCTION

"FEAR HATH TORMENT"

FRIENDLY READER: Are you, or have you ever been a believer in the doctrine of future endless punishment? And did you ever tremble with fearful apprehension that you might be irrevocably doomed to a life of interminable woe beyond the tomb? Did you ever shudder at the horrible thought, that either yourself or some of your dearest friends might possibly, in "the day of accounts," be numbered among those who are to receive the terrible sentence, "Depart from me, ye cursed, into everlasting fire, prepared for the Devil and his angels?" Matt. xxv: 41. Were you ever tormented and goaded with such fearful forebodings as these, and haunted with them day and night, for weeks and months together, if not during long and tedious years, as thousands upon thousands of the most devout believers in the Christian faith have been in all ages of the Church? Or were you ever present during a "religious revival," to witness the priest remove (in imagination) the cover from Hell's burning mouth (that blazing, "bottomless pit," whose lurid flames of fire "ascendeth up forever and ever"), and did you hear him depict to a terror-

11

stricken audience the awful fate of the countless millions of the "doomed, damned souls" of the underground world? Did you ever listen as he portrayed their agonizing sufferings, and spoke of their loud, terror-inspiring, heart-rending wailings of anguish, their woeful groans, their doleful yells and soul-bursting shrieks of despair, which, like a thousand commingling thunders, reverberating along the great archway of their murky prison, shook "Heaven, and Earth, and Hell?" And did a shuddering fear steal over your nerveless frame, and chill the blood in your very hearts in spite of your efforts to resist it and stave it off, as the "pulpit orator," in glowing eloquence, depicted the wretched inhabitants of this world of woe, as being tossed to and fro with their naked souls upon a fathomless sea of flame; a shoreless ocean of boiling, blazing, sulphurous fire, lashed into furious, dashing mountainous billows, by the ever thundering, ever bursting, never-ceasing storms of divine wrath? And as they essay to quench their parching thirst with this liquid fire, "the worm that never dies," robed in burning brimstone, we are told, makes his eternal feasts upon the vitals of their bleeding hearts, lacerated by the swift-sped thunderbolts of Jehovah's direful vengeance —aye, the barbed arrows, fresh drawn from God's own quiver! An old grim Lucifer, the deputed executor (in part) of God's vengeful wrath, heedless of their doleful yells and maddening cries, culminates the awful drama as he "woods up the fires and keeps them burning," and pours the red-hot, blistering embers down their shrieking throats!

A popular Christian clergyman, the Rev. Mr. D——, in a fit of inspirational turgescence and mental explosion, which recently came off in Xenia, Ohio, as he collapsed, let off the following: "Fathers and sons, *pastors* [mark this, ye preachers!] and people, husbands and wives, brothers and sisters, in unquenchable fire, with swollen veins and bloodshot eyes, strain toward each other's throats and hearts, reprobate men and women, devils in form and features, hideous to behold. As God's vengeance is in his heart, and he delights to execute it, he will tread them in his wrath and trample them in his fury, and he will stain all his garments with their blood! [Wonder if he will then reascend his burnished and beautiful "emerald throne" with these bloody clothes on.] My head grows dizzy, as it bends over the gulf!" [Quite likely, brother; lofty climbing always has the effect to make men with small brains giddy-headed. Empty vessels float easily. And we humbly suggest that you should have been cupped, blistered, bled, and put to bed instanter, and opiates and cooling powders administered *ad infinitum* after such an exhausting, moonstruck effort to scare sinners into Heaven.]

Take another example: A Rev. Mr. Clawson, a Methodist Episcopal clergyman, as "it came to pass," being once pregnant with the spirit of eternal damnation, and not knowing, as we suspect, "whether he was in the body or out of the body" (2 Cor ii: 4), blew up the *unconverted portion of his audience* in the following spasmodic style: "God will heap the red-hot cinders of black damnation upon your naked souls as high as the pyramids of Egypt." We suggest that Mrs. Partington would have considered this as rather a dangerous case of "*information* of the brain," or of "a rush of brains to the head."

Now, kind reader, let me ask you, have you had any practical experience in listening to such frightful and frightening ebullitions of folly and fanaticism as the foregoing, which we have presented here as mere specimens of the kind of priestly flummery which are continually rolling out from the pulpit upon the recurrence of every Sabbath, in every part of Christendom? Though it is true such pompous and foolish language is not always used as is found in the examples we have here presented, yet the spirit manifested is the same. And have you ever calculated or reflected upon the vast, untold and almost inconceivable amount of terror, fright, misery and despair, and consequent destruction of happiness it has brought to millions of minds and millions of families of the present era, as well as those of the remotely past superstitious ages? If so, you can understand our object and appreciate our motive in throwing this book before the public. For certain we are, that "in fear there is torment," and consequently unhappiness; and certain we are, too, that if the two hundred millions of people called Christians could be made acquainted with the historical facts which will be found in this work, and which go to prove most conclusively, that the doctrine of future endless punishment was originated and concocted by designing priests, and that a benevolent and beneficent God had nothing to do with their origination, as is claimed by the devout disciples of every primitive religion in the world, it would have the effect to dissipate a fathomless and shoreless ocean of fear and misery from the religious world. For it is now well known to every intelligent person, that the fear of endless damnation has been, and still is, a powerful engine in the hands of the priests for "converting souls to God"—*i.e.*, for grinding (or scaring) sinners into saints, and that there has always been at least ten devil-dreading, hell-fearing Christians to one that is made practically righteous by the natural love of virtue and truth. It is the fear of the Devil, and not the love of God,

which extorts from them a reluctant and tardy
conformity to the principles of justice and the
rules of practical honesty. That is, the Devil is
virtually set upon their track as a hound dog to
scare them into Heaven. And thus, they are
nothing less, properly speaking, than *drafted
saints,* or rather *pious sinners*—Christians by
practice, but villains at heart. And if they shall
receive the final benediction of "well done," it
will, we opine, have to be attributed more to a
pair of fleet legs than to a virtuous mind, for the
former achieve the work enabling them to out-run
"the grand adversary of souls," who howls upon
every Christian's track, "like a roaring lion, seeking whom he may devour." And here we may note
it as a remarkable fact, that as momentous and
solemnly important as this subject must be admitted to be, involving as it does our fate to all
eternity, yet not one pious Christian in a thousand
is able, when interrogated upon the subject, to
give an intelligent answer as to the origin of the
doctrine of *post mortem* punishment. (I have
never found one that could). They know nothing
about how, when or where it first started, and this
ignorance is sufficient to account for their blind
and tenacious adherence to the supersitition. It
is generally believed and assumed, that its primary source is the Christian Bible. And does not,
we ask, this lamentable ignorance greatly enhance

the necessity and importance of publishing and circulating a work of this character, that by virtue of superior knowledge, the people may be undeceived in supposing that it is of divine institution, instead of being, as history proves, of mundane priestly origin, and that they may thereby be delivered from the agonizing thraldom of fear and fright which have in all past ages beset the votaries of the various fear-fraught religions. If it were ever a wise policy to try to frighten men into the path of virtue by "the fear of Hell torments," as was ingeniously argued by the Grecian Polyarchists (300 B.C.), that policy is now superseded by the substitution of more honorable, more laudable, and more enduring motives.

THE BIOGRAPHY OF SATAN

CHAPTER 1

EVILS AND DEMORALIZING EFFECTS OF THE DOCTRINE
OF ENDLESS PUNISHMENT

"Grant me, great God, at least,
This one, this simple, almost no request:
When I have wept a thousand lives away,
When torment has grown weary of its prey;
When I have raved ten thousand years in fire—
Yea, ten thousand times ten thousand.
Let me then expire."

We have not space for an elaborate exposition of the evils and immoral effects of the doctrine of endless torment, but will present a brief list of a portion of them, condensed from our larger work on this subject, of which this work is an epitome or abstract:

1. The belief in a cruel after-death punishment is (as we have already shown) the prolific source, on their own account of groundless and tormenting fears to all its believers.

2. It is also the source of a fearful amount of the most painful unhappiness to millions of the human race in dread apprehension of the fate of their friends, even when but little is entertained on their own account.

3. The *post mortem* punishment doctrine taught by the Christian world, invests the Diety with a character absolutely dishonorable and disgraceful, if not blasphemous, by representing him as morally capable of inflicting the most excruciating punishment upon the major portion of his children, whereas he would be a cruel and hateful monster if he should thus punish one of his subjects for a single day.

4. It also fastens a disgraceful libel upon the moral attributes of man, by representing him as being so demon-hearted, even after he is translated to Heaven and numbered among "the spirits of the just men made perfect," that he can witness, unmoved, the intolerable sufferings and raving torments of the millions of his fellow beings, consigned to endless woe.

5. It has caused the butchery, the bloody slaughter of millions of the human race by the efforts used to convert them, and "the rest of mankind" to the true religion, in order to "save their souls from Hell."

6. It has caused numberless suicides, infanticides, fratricides, etc.; children have been murdered, for fear they would lead a life of crime, and thus "plunge their souls into Hell."

7. The belief in Devil obsession and endless punishment has caused more than one hundred thousand human beings to be tortured to death in

various ways by "Christians" who believed in the superstitious notion of witchcraft.

8. The belief in *post mortem* punishment was the great "*motor nerve*," the primary mainspring of the Spanish Inquisition in which "Christians" slaughtered, and "sent to the bar of God," more than forty thousand men, women and children.

9. It was the foundation of the fiendish war of the Crusades, in which *five millions* of people were made to drench the earth with their blood by the hands of "Christians."

10. It has contributed to fill our lunatic asylums with the insane, made so in many instances by the awful thought of eternal damnation.

11. It has caused an enormous expenditure of time and money in the various means used (as books, tracts, sermons, etc.), for propagating the doctrine.

12. And finally, it converts the Christian world into cowards, instead of moral heroes, by appealing solely to the organ of fear—the basest of human motives—instead of to the natural love of virtue implanted in the human mind.

We have an abundance of historical facts in our possession to prove all the above statements, but can not occupy space with many of them in this small work. With reference to the first objection in the list, as also the third and fourth, the lines quoted from the poet Young furnish us illustrative proof. The victim of endless damnation prays that "After I have raved ten thousand years in fire, let me then expire." But the Christian world tells us God answers, "No sir; your raving torments shall never, never have an end!" Now, not only must such doctrine as this be appalling to weak nerves, but we regard it as virtual blasphemy, as it represents God as being a more demon-hearted, inhuman monster than the most bloody-minded tyrant that ever drenched the earth with human blood! For neither Nero nor Caligula ever attempted to punish and torture, in the most cruel manner imaginable, even his bitterest enemy for a year, much less an eternity, as God is here represented as doing.

But more and worse. Listen to the following, from one of the most popular promulgators of the Christian faith that ever *graced*, or rather *disgraced*, the land of Christendom:

The Rev. J. Edwards, a very popular preacher of the last century, president of a theological seminary in New Jersey, and "one of the brightest luminaries of the Christian Church," as Rev. Robert Hall styles him, proclaimed from the sacred desk, that "the elect (in heaven) will not be sorry for the damned (in Hell). It will cause no uneasiness or dissatisfaction to them, but on the contrary, when they see this sight, it will occasion

rejoicing, and excite them to joyful praises."
("Edward's Practical Sermons," No. 11).

Now, reader, keep down "the old man," restrain your feelings of horror till we present you
another example of this kind:

The Rev. Nathaniel Emmons, who quit the
stage of time in 1840, once declared in a sermon,
that "the happiness of the elect will consist in
part in witnessing the torments of the damned in
Hell, among whom may be their own children,
parents, husbands, wives and friends; . . . but instead of taking the part of these miserable beings,
they will say, 'Amen, hallelujah, praise the
Lord.' "

Now, assuming this to be Christian doctrine,
who will not blush to be called a Christian? But
perhaps some reader will reply that it is not—
that it is *bogus* Christianity. Then we ask him to
explain, how Heaven can be "a place or state of
perpetual happiness" (see Webster's Dictionary),
unless its inhabitants can witness such scenes as
these unmoved. If "perpetually happy," they
must actually enjoy every scene they witness.
And hence must shout, "Amen, hallelujah, praise
the Lord," when witnessing, as they do according
to the Scriptures (Luke xvi: 23), their friends
and relatives, rolling, raving and shrieking with
the pangs of perpetual woe.

Now, reader, don't you see that Edwards and

Emmons were preaching the genuine Christian doctrines? Whether or not, however, we regard such sentiments not only as blasphemous caricatures upon a just and benevolent God, but as insulting libels upon human nature as it exists among "the spirits of the just made perfect." If our friends, after entering Paradise, did really possess such a character as here ascribed to them, I would rather be a dog and bark at the moon to all eternity, even though I should be endowed with the perpetual charter or special privilege of singing "Old Hundred," or playing on "the harp of a thousand strings" forever and ever. And sermous containing just such gospel rantings as these may be found in nearly every Christian library in the world, exerting a demoralizing influence on all who read and believe them.

CHAPTER II

We now propose to submit to the reader a brief and condensed history of the ancient notions respecting the origin and infernal operations and machinations of that imaginary monster, counter-foe and arch-enemy to all human bliss and blessedness, known as "the Devil," "Satan," "the Serpent," "the Dragon," etc.; but for whom we think a more appropriate designation would be, "The Rival of Omnipotence," or "Omnipotence Second."

Here let the reader note it and emphasize it as a remarkable fact, *that God, not the Devil, was primarily believed to be the author of evil*, by the Oriental nations, and *that this doctrine is taught in the Christian Bible*. The words *Evil* and *Devil* seem to have been originally synonymous terms, the latter being, as we are told, a contraction of the words "do-evil," and hence represents a mere personification of evil. And there is abundance of evidence accessible to prove that the conception of evil existed long before the Devil was discovered or thought of; so that should his Devilish majesty set up a claim, or any of his friends for

25

him as being the originator or author of evil, he
would be non-suited in open court. The case
would be reduced to a *nolle prosequi,* or pronounced *tout au contraire.* Instead of ascribing
evil to the Devil in the early ages of human
society, we find it was ascribed to the Deity himself, and considered the natural action of his own
faculties, the normal and divine powers and purposes. He was assumed to be the source of both
good and evil. There being already (in the conception of the people) one Infinite Being (God),
no room was found in the original creation for another, and hence his sooty majesty was left out.
He was an after-thought. It was not until the
second edition of creation was struck off, that his
long-tailed lordship was thought of, or allowed
to have any existence except among snakes. He
was finally gotten up as a "helpmeet" for the
priests, it being discovered that it would require
the three-fold power: first, of "the drawing
chords of love" from the fountain of infinite goodness; second, the draw-game of the priests (upon
the pockets of the people), and, third, the howling
of the Serpent, *alias* the Dragon, *alias* the Devil
(like "a roaring lion"), to get a sinner into
Heaven.

Verily, verily, "Jordan is a hard road to travel,
I believe"—*i.e.,* Heaven seems to be a place not
very accessible.

We have stated that the Devil was not thought of in the original creation, and how the people were restrained from the commission of universal crime and carnage without the fear of the imaginary ghost of old king Beelzebub before their eyes, is a "mystery of godliness," which we suppose only the spiritually-minded can comprehend —that is, those who are sufficiently spiritually-minded to "understand the things that belong to the kingdom," or to see a Devil where there is none.

There is abundance of historical testimony to prove that no nation in its earlier history—not even "God's holy people," had any idea or conception of the existence of a prime originator of evil, or "tempter of souls," separate and apart from God himself, while it is evident that no possible advantage or end could have been served by the existence of such a being, while the people were ignorant of it and the conception foreign to their thoughts. Hence the presumption must be, that he was not yet born or hatched. Strange, too, when according to orthodox showing, that was an age of the world in which it was all-important and indispensably necessary that he should have been incoronated and established upon his throne, and the fact extensively advertised, because we are told that "the imagination of man's heart is evil from his youth"—Gen. viii: 21—

and, hence, a Devil was needed to scare them on the right track—"the strait and narrow way that leadeth unto Jordan," as we are virtually taught this is his "high calling," the great end of his creation. It certainly, then, was a great blunder, a serious desideratum, to omit his creation at the start, or if created, to neglect to make it known. Good and evil were primarily regarded as only different degrees of the same thing, and both as emanations from an all-wise and perfect God, "the author of everything, both good and bad," whose residence then by many was believed to be the sun. And let it be noted here that the first conception of evil and a Devil was inferred from the violent and destructive operations of the elements of nature not now classified with, or regarded by any one as moral evils, and which it was known that human beings could have no agency in producing. And here dates the first rude conception of a Devil, which means simply a destroyer—not of souls, but of natural objects.

CHAPTER III

The proof that the early Jews (Hebrews or Israelites, rather), like the heathen at a still earlier period, were entirely ignorant of, and had no conception of, the existence of a Devil, or distinct evil principle, and ascribed all evil and all crime, as well as all goodness, to God, is of a threefold character.

1. The absence of any allusion to such a personage in the Jewish Scriptures, or even to a state of punishment after death.

2. The repeated positive declarations in the same "Holy Book," that God himself is the author of evil.

3. The fact that all those names, terms and titles now applied to the Devil, or used to designate such a being, found in the Old Testament, were by the Jews applied also to God, and are still more remotely traceable to Pagan astronomical imagery or star-born spiritual beings.

First. Relative to the first of these propositions, it may be remarked, that orthodox Christians have often been challenged to place a finger upon a single text in the Jewish Old Testament

(the only authentic record of their doctrine),
which either specially or by fair implication
teaches the existence of either a Devil or an endless Hell, or any doctrine tantamount thereto

If we examine the history of the first transgression ever committed by man, according to the
Jewish and Christian Scriptures, we will find no
allusion to these doctrines, and no threat of punishment in another life as a penalty for this or any
other sin, as most certainly we should, if these
doctrines were then known, believed and propa-
gated. True, we are told that Mother Eve was
beguiled by a serpent to eat an apple. But a serpent is not a Devil, according to our dictionaries,
but a snake. And according to the opinion of the
learned Dr. Adam Clarke, the serpent that beguiled Eve was really nothing more nor less than
an ape or monkey—a very different animal
(having a tail and destructive propensities) from
the fancied cloven-footed Orthodox Devil. But
whether the original tempter were a Devil, serpent, snake, snapping-turtle, or biped, quadru-
ped, nonruped, or a legless, crawling reptile, there
is no intimation that he had anything to do with
punishing Adam and his wife for their "manifold
transgressions," but let them slide over Jordan
unmolested. There is no account that either of
them were consigned to the fiery pit, minus a bottom; no sentence or threat of never-ending tor-

ment or punishment beyond the grave as penalty for the first great transgression of the human race —that "mighty sin" which resulted, we are told, in the downfall, depravity, and almost moral wreck and ruin of the entire race of man. Now, had there been a Devil then "to punish the wicked," certainly he would have been brought out, sworn into office, and put upon duty. His enthronement and inauguration would not have been delayed an hour. At least his existence and his fiery whereabouts would have been proclaimed "from Dan to Beersheba," and Jehovah's threatening vengeance and thunderbolts of wrath would have been rolled in fiery billows, along the moral heavens as he announced the existence of a world of endless woe for all sinners and apple eaters in the future, as well as the place of consignment for Father Adam and his new rib-made wife for ruining the human race, by indulging their gustatory proclivities upon a pippin. The existence of a fiery world, with its malignant, restless ruler and omnipotent potentate, should have been and would have been announced, and the notice engraven in imperishable golden characters upon the boundless, cerulean, over-arching concave of Heaven, immediately after the first transgression of man, as a standing terror and eternal warning to sinners, or those who might be tempted to sin, in order to deter them from future transgression and future crime, had such penal arrangements existed or been thought of. But instead of this, the punishment was only temporal. The ground was cursed, Grandmother Eve sentenced to "bring forth children in sorrow," the serpent doomed when hungry to eat dust (except in wet weather, when he had to "go it slyly," if not suffocatingly, on mud), and Grandfather Adam chased out of the garden "with a sharp stick," but no roasting or fiery pit punishment is even once named.

Second. Then look at the case of the first commission of the greatest crime ever perpetrated by human hands, or ever registered upon the scroll of human depravity—that of the perpetration of murder, and the murder, too, of a brother (fratricide). Cain was to be a "fugitive and a vagabond in the earth," for killing his brother, and the soil was to be unpropitious on his account. But there is no burning, broiling or frying threatened, or hinted at, to be inflicted either in this life or "that which is to come."

Third. Not even on the occasion of issuing "the law on Mount Sinai," when we must presume the whole counsel of God was proclaimed, and when it is confessed the whole world was steeped in crime, do we find the doctrine of future rewards and punishments in another life even hinted at.

Fourth. Nor yet on the occasion of drowning the whole world for its superlative wickedness (Noah and family only excepted), was the fiery whereabouts of the "Evil One"—his Satanic Snakeship—made known and announced as the future home of the wicked. There is no intimation, that while their bodies should be floating on the expansive waters of the "mighty deep," their souls should be roasting in pandemonium below, or should be floating on a sea of fire. Noah was a "preacher of righteousness," but not a preacher of "endless damnation."

Fifth. We will dismiss the argument with the remark, that while Jehovah is represented as often getting angry, and as being again and again engaged in dealing out his fulminating thunders upon his "holy people"—in pouring out his threats, curses and wrathful imprecations upon the "devoted heads of his own chosen nation," he never once threatened them with fire and brimstone, or to cast them into the pit without a bottom, for their "numerous transgressions," their "manifold backslidings," and their "wickedness of heart," not even after they had rolled up a mountain of crime, whose towering apex stood in defiant mockery before the throne of Heaven. Two thousand five hundred years thus rolled away after creation, as we have shown (and we will now add to it at least one thousand more, basing our calculation on "Jude's Christian Chronology"), before his Devilish or Snakish Majesty was born or ushered upon the stage of action; or, at least, before he was introduced to society, or anybody was honored with his acquaintance, or even suspected his existence. As we find no traces of him among the prophets, he either had led a very obscure and retired life, or was yet in the labyrinths of chaos. For it was not until about the dawning of the era of the Gospel Dispensation, that he was inaugurated and crowned king of pandemonium by the Christian world.

Now we have only to appeal to the Jewish and Christian history to show that society was as moral, and as free from crime, during this long period, that the world (or at least this portion of it) was in want of a "Devil" to help on the cause of Zion, as during the Devil-preaching, Hell-scaring system or policy of proclaiming the Gospel, and frightening the people into piety and Paradise (or rather into priest-paying pews), which was practiced in the "dark ages," so called. If then, society could prosper without a Devil for nearly four thousand years, why could it not continue to prosper without his assistance or presence through all time to come? More especially as we have the historical proof that society was not improved morally by his introduction into the world, or the introduction among the people of the belief in such a being, as we could amply prove, and as is well known to every reader of history. Hence, is it not evident, that as there was no "prime evil agent" known to society in the early ages, to assume the introduction of one after the lapse of several thousand years, is to assume that in the economy of God something took place which was entirely useless, redundant, foolish and absurd. Reader, please answer this question before you read further. Tell us why it *now* requires two omnipotent powers (God and the Devil) to save a sinner or get a Christian into heaven—one leading the way with the inviting language, "Come, ye blessed of my Father," the other pursuing in the rear, howling upon his track like a roaring lion, when but one was sufficient during a period of four thousand years. Reader, reason and reflect.

CHAPTER IV

I have asserted what I will here repeat, that the primitive Jews did not teach the doctrines of a Devil and a Hell, as appertaining to another life. It can not be found in the Old Testament, nor in any writings of the Jews prior to the Babylonian captivity (600 years B.C.), during which some of the Jewish sects obtained these doctrines. Let it not be supposed that I am ignorant of the fact that the words, "Devils" (always in the plural) and "Hell," occur several times in the Old Testament, but they are never used in the sense now popularly attached to these words. In every instance in which they are employed, they have exclusive reference to this life. It should be specially noted that the word Devil never occurs in the Old Testament. It is always in the plural—"Devils," and in this form had reference either to heathen deities, or to the evil spirits which many of the Jews believed infested the minds of men in this life. They had no "king Satan," or "prime Devil," as they had no place to keep him—no bottomless pit of fire and sulphur to cast him into. As for the word Hell where it occurs in the

36

Old Testament, it is translated and derived in every instance from *sheol*, and *sheol* is the Hebrew word for grave. And it is a noteworthy fact, that it is translated grave in twenty-eight cases. Why it was not translated grave in other cases, and in all instances where it is found in the Old Testament, is a "mystery of godliness," which will hereafter be explained. But the context and the original meaning of the word "Hell," where it is found in the Old Testament, clearly shows that it would have made better sense had it been translated "grave." I will here present some proof of this. Job ejaculates "Oh, that thou wouldst hide me in the grave!" (*sheol*). Job xiv: 13. David exclaims: "If I make my bed in Hell (*sheol*), behold, thou art there!" (Psalm cxxxix: 8).

Observe how much similiarity of sense exists in the two texts above quoted. And yet the former is translated grave, and the latter, Hell. Now, why did the translators render *sheol* Hell in the latter, instance, so as to make David talk of making his bed in Hell? Who that has an ounce of brains between his ears would speak or think of making his bed in a cauldron of blazing fire and brimstone, or a red-hot furnace of living coals glowing with the most intense heat? He could not "sleep a wink" in a month in such a situation. But had *sheol* in this text been translated grave instead of Hell, it would read, "If I make my bed in the grave," etc., language which approaches much nearer to good sense, for the grave will really be our bed when our bodies are consigned to the earth. I ask, then, which is the most reasonable translation, Hell or grave? Again, Jonah is made to say: "Out of the belly of Hell cried I, and thou heardest me." (Jonah ii: 2.) What! Did Jonah tumble through "Symme's Hole" into Tartarus (for he was too righteous a man to be driven thither) unobserved by Omniscience, who was not apprized of the sad catastrophe till the prophet roared and bellowed with a voice sufficiently stentorian to be heard over the "wailings of the damned," all the way from the "belly of Hell up to the throne of Heaven."

How did his Jonahship get loose from the clutches of old Splitfoot, grizzly king, Beelzebub? Or how did he manage to elude the vigilant watch of his jail-keeper, old Tisiphon, who guards the gates of Cerebus "day and night," so as to dodge through the door and make his way back to Nineveh? There were no Isaac T. Hoppers in Pandemonium then to construct underground railroads, and run off some of the "damned souls" occasionally. The truth is, Jonah's "belly of Hell" was the belly of a whale—a pretty warm place, but not as hot as boiling brimstone—not hot enough to singe the hair or burn a blister.

It is evident, therefore, that *sheol* here is inappropriately translated Hell; and it would not have been so translated, but that, as a Christian once expressed the idea, "It would not do to have no Hell and Devil in the Old Testament." His feelings were analogous to those of the Methodist Episcopal clergyman, who exclaimed to his congregation: "Brethren, the Universalists tell us all men are to be saved; but we do not believe it. *We hope for better things.*" Let it not be understood, however, that those who translated *sheol* into Hell, entertained the thought that it had reference to any other than this life. Some of them have admitted that it had no reference to another state of being. I venture to affirm that no Hebrew scholar would risk his reputation for learning by interpreting *sheol* as having reference to a place of torment after death. They all know better. Commentators skilled in the language and in Jewish history, admit this is not the true interpretation, and the context proves it. All Jewish history shows that they never in their earlier history had any conception of a Devil or Hell as being provided or prepared for the wicked in another state of existence.

A volume might easily be furnished of historical extracts from some of the best and most popular authors, both Jewish and Christian, in proof of this statemnt, but a few must suffice:

The celebrated Christian Church historian, Mr. Milman, declares that "the lawgiver, Moses, maintained a profound silence on that fundamental article, if not of political at least of religious legislation—rewards and punishments in another life."—"History of Jews," vol. i, p, 117.

Bishop Warburton, so well known in English Church history, and whom a writer, Mr. Arnold, styles "a great and shining ornament of the Gallican Church," says: "In the Jewish republic, both rewards and punishments promised by heaven were temporal only, such as health, long life, peace, plenty and dominion, etc. (on the one hand), and disease, premature death, war, famine, captivity, etc. (on the other). In no one place of the Mosaic Institute, is there the least mention, or any intelligent hint, of the rewards and punishments of another life."—"Divine Legislation," vol. iii, p. 2.

"No mention is anywhere made in the writings of Moses of a judgment day at the end of the world," says Mr. Mayer, Professor of the Dutch Reformed Church. And that great logical defender of the Christian faith, Dr. Paley, avers to the same effect, that "the Mosaic Dispensation dealt in temporal rewards and punishments, and you observe that these blessings consisted altogether of worldly benefits, and the curses of worldly punishment."—Sermon xii, p. 10.

Bishop Watson, the champion defender of the Christian faith against Paine's "Age of Reason," tells us that devils in the Old Testament means "men and women as traducers." The learned and celebrated Dr. Campbell says, relative to the word *sheol* which is rendered hell in several places in our translation of the Old Testament, that "it sometimes signifies the state of the dead without regard to their happiness or misery," as the Religious Encyclopædia of England tells us the Jews had a conception of a world or place of general rendezvous for souls after death without distinction of character.

The ablest and most popular Christian scholars, then, admit that the early Jews, known primarily as Hebrews, had no conception of a personified wicked agent, or transmundane personal Devil, or of a place of endless torment beyond the confines of time; but that all words or names in the Old Testament, seemingly implying such ideas, were intended to have reference exclusively to this sphere of being.

CHAPTER V

Our next and second proposition is, that the earliest ancestors of the Jewish race recognized God as being the author of evil by virtue of being the source of everything. The sequence had to be admitted to maintain a logical consistency. God could not be the author of all things without being the author of evil. The doctrine of future rewards and punishments constituted no part of the ancient Jewish creed, simply because, as we would naturally infer, all human actions, both good and bad, were regarded as proceeding from their God, Jehovah, or as being "inspired by the great Breath," as they express it (in the Talmud). But we are not left to mere inference from the omission of after-life punishment for wrong-doing from their creed, that they regarded God as the author of evil—but we have it taught in the most explicit and unequivocal language in their own "Inspired Writings." Read and mark well this inspired utterance of the great and leading prophet of the Jews, "I form light and create darkness. I make peace, and I *create evil.* I, the Lord, do all these things" (Isaiah). Could language be more explicit than this? And the prophet Amos asks, "Shall there be evil in the city, and the Lord hath not done it?" And Job speaks in the same strain, and puts forth the same doctrine: "We receive good at the hands of the Lord, shall we not also receive evil?" And Solomon also carries the principle or doctrine so far as to declare, "the Lord hath made even the wicked for the doing of evil," as it should read: but our translation makes it read, "the day of evil." Let it not be said that it is merely physical evils that are referred to in these texts for, besides these, there are numerous other texts which go to show that there was not a crime known or perpetrated at that day, but what Jehovah himself is represented as committing or approving, and thereby assuming the authorship of it. For example, he puts a lying spirit into the mouths of the prophets (see 1 Kings, 22), so that all the falsehoods they told were his, and not theirs. And the prophet Jeremiah goes further, and says that God lied virtually with his own lips: "Wilt thou be altogether to me as a liar?" "O Lord, thou hast deceived me, and I am greatly deceived" (Jer. xxii: 7). And Ezekiel caps the climax: "If a prophet is deceived I the Lord have deceived that prophet." Now as deception and falsehood are synonymous terms it follows that God stands charged here

with being a liar, *i.e.*, "the father of lies" in the
Jewish system, as the Devil was afterwards in the
Christian system.   He is frequently represented
as getting mad (Deut. i: 37), and swearing; and
also of committing or approving of theft or
stealing (Ex. iii: 2), of robbery (Ex. xii: 36), of
murder (Deut. xiii: 2), and in fact of every crime
known in that barbarous age.

Now, it is easy to perceive from this, why the
Jews had no Devil.   They had nothing for him to
do.   The Lord did it all.   He perpetrated the evil
as well as achieved the good.   And to punish
the wicked or evil-doer with "everlasting fire,"
would have been to build a fire around their God.
And let us here remark, that optimism (the belief
that everything is ordered for the best) is a doctrine scouted by the Christian Church—yet it certainly is the legitimate inference from the above
quoted texts from their own sacred Bible.

Of course, if every species of crime, evil and
immorality, had the divine sanction, it was all
right—*ergo*, it was for the best.   Nor is it incredi-
ble that the Jews in a state of barbarism, and
mental childhood, should have no clear conception of a line of demarkation between good and
evil, and hence confound and classify them all
together.   The oldest books in the Hindoo Bible
evince the same state of mind, and also teach the
same doctrine.

CHAPTER VI

GOD AND THE DEVIL ORIGINALLY TWIN-BROTHERS, AND KNOWN BY THE SAME TITLES

Another proof that the primitive Jews, like some of the earlier heathen nations, had no Devil, and recognized but one common source for good and evil, regarding both as proceeding from Jehovah, is found in the fact that those names and titles now applied to the Devil, were by them and other nations primarily applied to the Deity, thus evidencing that both characters were formerly comprehended in one being, that being Jehovah—God; and that after another being (the Devil) was hatched, created or conjured up to saddle all the sins of the world on, he still continued to be known and designated by the same names and titles that various nations, including Jews, had used in application to God only; whereas a being possessing opposite characteristics should have been designated by a name denoting opposite qualities. The fact is clear (as we shall soon show) that the Devil was at first considered a God, and as such was worshiped by several nations including some of the early Christian sects. And the same is true of Jesus Christ and the Devil, that the same titles were applied to each, an evi-

dence that they were both derived in common
from the Pagan conception of good and evil,
virtue and vice flowing or emanating from the
same fountain, which fountain was primordially
the sun. In Exodus, 6, God is represented as
saying, "I appeared unto Abraham, unto Isaac,
and unto Jacob, as God Almighty." Now this
God Almighty is found to read in the Hebrew
Bible, Baal-Shadai, and in tracing the derivation
of Beelzebub, the highest title for our or "your
father the Devil," to its original analytic form, we
find it terminate in Baal-Shadai. Thus both are
traceable to the same origin. Beelzebub, in its
original Chaldean and Phœnician form is Baalzebub. Then we have Baal-Shadai *God Almighty*,
and Baalzebub the *Devil*. And on further research, we find these terms are essentially the
same—that is, were originally applied to the same
being. Baal, as synonymous with Bel, was the
Chaldean name for the Lord dwelling in the sun.
Baal-Shadai was the sun in the zenith of his glory,
and Baalzebub the sun while in the sign or
constellation of the scorpion. And then there is
Baal-ial, or Baal-iel, a Chaldean and Phœnician
solar title for God. And this is the word or term
from which the Devilish Beliel of the Christian
New Testament is derived. Beliel is from Baal-
iel, Lord of the Opposite, which means a sign or
constellation opposite to the sun at any given

point. Adversary, another Satanic title ("your adversary the Devil." 1 Peter, 5-8), is also traceable to the same source; Adversary being like Beliel a sign at right-angles, or adverse (adversary) to the sun. Paul asks, "What concord hath Christ with Beliel?" I answer, the same that Christ hath with the Father, all being traceable to one and the same original source. Dragon is another title for the great Attorney General of the lower kingdom, and is found to be synonymous with Baal and Bel. St. John speaks of "that old Serpent which is called the Devil and Satan—the great Red Dragon, with seven heads and ten horns, and a tail which drew the third part of the stars of heaven, and cast them to the earth" (Rev. xii, xiii). Here Serpent, Devil, Satan and Dragon, are used as synonymous terms, as nouns in apposition. Now, let it be observed, that the Dragon was worshiped by the Canaanites under the name of Dagon, and Dagon is compounded of Dag, *the fish,* and On or One, the Egyptian name for the God of the sun or in the sun. And this On or One is the source to which "The Holy *One*" of Israel is traceable. Dragon or Dagon, then, signifies Dag, the *fish,* and On or One, the sun—that is the sun in the constellation of the fish. Satan, another of the numerous epithets or titles, with which His Cloven-footed Majesty was honored or dubbed is from the Babylonian Saith-

ain or Aith-ain, and is said to mean *The Word
Logos,* Fountain of Wisdom, etc. If, then, Satan is the founder of wisdom, there is some sense
and appropriateness, after all, in the Scripture
injunction, "Be ye wise as serpents (or satans),
and harmless as doves." And some consistency,
too, may be found, according to this explanation
of Satan, in the two apparently incongruous Scripture texts—one representing God and the other
Satan as tempting David to number the people.
It may seem like a *dernier* expedient to get rid of
a glaring contradiction—to make God and the
Devil both one. But perhaps the end will sancti-
fy the means; and if truth is sometimes stranger
than fiction, may it not be in this instance?

Another title, applied to both God and the
Devil, is that of Father. Christ spoke of "My
Father in Heaven," and "your Father, the
Devil." "Ye are of your Father, the Devil."
(John vii: 44). He also referred to a certain class
of believers, crying "Abba, Father." Well, now,
Abba, we are informed, is from the Abaddon,
(Abad-don), which St. John tells us is the Hebrew
for Beelzebub, while Apollyon, (Latin, Apollo) is
the Greek (Rev. ix). Apollo is, however, the
Latin, for the impersonal Sun, Solar God. Abba
is Father, and Don is Lord in the Hebrew, and
according to the inspired John, the Revelator, the
two together is Beelzebub. Abba-don-Father-

Lord-Beelzebub—rather an imposing title for his Snakeship.

We will now notice some of the titles in common to Christ and the Devil. Lucifer (suggestive of Lucifer matches, of which it may be presumed his Satanship was the patentee or inventor), if not a common title for the "Evil One," is, at least a very illustrious title. I think the old gentleman was formerly better known by this title than at present. It is one of the numerous titles, however, by which he has always been known and honored. Isaiah dubs his Royal Majesty as "Lucifer, Son of the morning" (Isaiah xiv: 12), or as some translators have it, and ours so explain it in the margin—Day Star. Then Lucifer was "Son of the Day Star." Well, now, mark the evidence. In Rev. xxii: 16, it reads: "I Jesus, am the bright and Morning Star." Then, there is just the difference between Lucifer and Jesus that there is between the Morning Star and the Day Star—which Bailey's Astronomy, and Dupois' "Astronomy of the Ancients," show to be none at all. They were one and the same Star. And this identity in the name of Christ and Lucifer, as well as the reasonableness of designating each a *star*, is rendered more apparent when we recollect that both were considered the source of light.

Christ was "a Light to Lighten the Gentiles"

(Luke ii:32). And Lucifer, or Satan, was by transformation "an Angel of Light" (II Cor. ix:15), or as it is rendered, "a Star of Light"— the stars anciently being considered angels, or the homes of angels, and were sometimes addressed as angels. We have then Christ as the "Morning Star," "Light to Lighten," etc., and Satan or Lucifer, "a Star of Light." Both are stars and both are lights. God is another honorable designation for both Christ and Satan. Christ is "The God of Peace" (II Cor. xiii:11), and Satan "The God of this world" (II Cor. iv:4). And the appropriateness of the designation, and validity of the title of the latter, I believe is not disputed by the Christian world. Christ himself seems to have conceded it; for when his Satanship offered him "all the kingdoms of this world" for one genuflection, or act of worship, he did not dispute his title, contest his proprietorship, or call in question the correctness of his boundless claim to "all the kingdoms of this world." He seemed disposed to "give the Devil his due," if not a little more.

Again, was Christ honored with the title of a "Prince?" So was the ruler of the brimstone kingdom. Christ was "The Prince of Peace"— Satan, "The Prince of Darkness," "The Prince of the Power of the Air." But why was he styled "The Prince of Darkness?" Do fire and

brimstone give no light? Certainly they do.
Then, would there not be as much propriety in
dubbing him "The Prince of Light," as an "Angel of Light?" However he is acknowledged to
be a "Prince" as well as Christ, and thus far
they are co-equal.

And did Christ receive the awe-imposing title
of "Son of God?" So did Satan receive a similar title. For "Son of the Morning" is, when
properly rendered, "Son of the God who made
the morning—who rules the morning," the God in
the sun. But, perhaps, the most common title,
or rather emblem for "that old serpent, the Devil," as John the Saint styles him, is that of a serpent. And serpent was a popular emblem
among the Jews for God also, if not a direct and
explicit title for the Deity. We are told (in Num.
xxi: 9), that "Moses made a serpent of brass,
and put it upon a pole, and it came to pass that
if a serpent had bitten any man, when he beheld
the serpent of brass he lived." Now we have the
most conclusive evidence that this serpent was designed to represent Jehovah. In the first place,
its uniform use in nearly all countries to represent
the Deity or the Devil, would indicate that
Moses' serpent was designed to represent one or
the other. And then, when Christ tells us that
Moses lifted up the serpent in the wilderness as
a type of him (Christ), we are no longer left in

doubt as to which of the two (God or the Devil) it was intended to represent, and constitute an image of. No doubt remains of its being intended as an image or emblem of Deity, especially when we take into consideration the wonderful and God-like healing power ascribed to it, equal to that of the great idol, Dagon of the Babylonians, than which it certainly was no less an idol. Certainly it would be difficult to conceive of a deeper vein of idolatry running through the religion or mythological system of any nation, than that practically manifested or implied in this brazen serpent of Moses, or brazen image of God, as we may truthfully style it. I think no greater power was ever ascribed to any idol nor more distinctly essential attributes of Deity. Then observe, what a glaring and high handed infraction it involves of the first commandment: "Thou shall not make unto thyself any graven image, nor the likeness of any thing that is in heaven above or in the earth beneath, or in the waters under the earth." Was not this brazen figure a likeness of something both "in the earth beneath," and "in the waters under the earth?" Are not serpents numerous in both localities? They were especially so at that time. I ask then what does the setting up of the serpent image by Moses lack of constituting idolatry, and commandment breaking but the name?

The origin of this brazen serpent's business among the Jews, however, is not hard to trace out. The Egyptians, among whom they dwelt for several hundred years, entertained a very high respect, and we say for a portion of them, veneration for serpents, as did other Pagan nations, and made much use of them as emblems in their religious worship; as did also the Persians among whom the Jews or Israelites long sojourned. The system of serpent worship was prevalent at that time in nearly every nation on the earth—that is, so far as to use and venerate them as emblems of God and his various attributes. And the reasons which led to the election of serpents for these purposes are also easily explained. It was simply because its peculiar form or construction and character made it susceptible of applying a great variety of emblems for most of the supposed leading attributes of the Deity.

We will here endeavor to present a brief explanation of the matter. In the first place, his entire wholeness or unitary construction of body being without limbs or external parts, suggested the serpent as an appropriate emblem of the unitary conception of the Godhead. And then his movement without feet or legs, thus making no noise, was suggestive of many noiseless, yet stupendous achievements of the Deity constantly going on throughout the Universe, as well as his supposed power to change his location without walking, without the use of feet and legs. And especially did this represent, in imagination, that beautiful, noiseless revolution of the planets, in their orbits, yet all the time observable to the devout worshiper—these shining orbs being venerable and sacred as the homes of the lesser gods. And the innumerable, shining, dazzling scales of the serpent, following, as he moved silently onward those two brilliant, visual orbs situated in the front of his head, were suggestive of the sun and moon leading the starry host through the heavens. By putting the end of his tail in his mouth, he formed a circle which was the chosen emblem of eternity. Mr. Higgins says, "The serpent was the emblem of eternity and immortality, and hence tempted the woman (in paradise) to bring forth immortal offspring."

This was the doctrine taught in some of the very ancient religions and mythologies, and revives very forcibly the story of Adam and Eve, and the serpent in Eden. The typical or emblematical use of the serpent to represent immortality, was suggested by the annual casting off the epidermis. The annual shedding of the skin of the serpent, which, however, always left him in possession of a new external covering, led many to believe that he never died, but was simply renewed or "regenerated," and born again every year, while all could see in the process an illustration of the soul's casting off the body in the act of being born into immortal life. Hence its use to represent eternity and immortality. The hissing of the serpent, it appears, was supposed or fancied to resemble "the still small voice of God."

The Jewish prophet, Isaiah, seems to have entertained this superstitious, Pagan idea when he declared, "The Lord will hiss unto them from the ends of the earth, and he will hiss for the fly of Egypt." This sounds rather snakish as well as heathenish. And Christ's "still small voice" was doubtless derived from this serpentine source as a "still voice" and a "small voice" were ascribed to the serpent.

And more than all, the wonderful attractions or fascinating power of the serpent was beautifully suggestive of "the drawing chords of love," which God was supposed to exercise towards all men. Christ declared, "If I be lifted up (like Moses' serpent in the wilderness), I will draw all men unto me." In like manner did Moses' serpent draw men unto it, and all natural serpents do likewise when men present themselves within the sphere of their magical powers. And by nearly every Oriental nation reported in history, the serpent was supposed to possess wonderful sanative powers. We are informed that the Egyptians were strong in this conception; and of them in all probability, Moses (who was "skilled in all the learning of the Egyptians," Acts vii: 22), borrowed the leading idea of his brazen serpent to heal the snake-bitten Israelites. And we are told the Hindoos and Grecians, as a portion of the Egyptian nation, were, from a very early period of their history, in the habit of carrying a pole, during their travels, with a serpent entwined around it. It will be recollected that Moses' brass serpent was constructed upon a pole. And the emblem of the healing God Esculapius, according to Faber, was a serpent around a pole.

The word seraphim, denoting an order of angels in the Hebrew theocracy (see Isaiah vi: 2— 6), and the word Serapis, the name of an Egyptian God, both appear to be derived from a serpent, and hence may be considered twin-brothers. And it is a singular circumstance, and one which must certainly be regarded as implying great veneration for the reptile or snakish tribe, that Moses' foster-mother (Thermuthis), according to Josephus, was named for a serpent—at least the Egyptians had a serpent by that name. We are told that the Hottentots from time immemorial have believed that bruising the head of the serpent with the heel will cure its bite, which calls to mind the seed of the woman bruising the serpent's head, as spoken of in Genesis iii. We have already elsewhere stated, that Eve is from Heiva, Heva, or Eva, a serpent. And we may state here that some of the early Christians partook of this spirit of universal homage paid to snakes or serpents. One of the earliest sects of Christian faith noticed in history, was called Ophiates (which is from Ophis, a serpent), on account of the homage then paid to serpents.

We are also informed, that more than a thousand years ago, Christians were in the habit of carrying serpents with them in their travels in the manner we have described some of the Pagan nations as doing. And the walls of some of their oldest churches may now be seen decorated with the figures of serpents. So that even the Christian religion seems to have been a little snakish or serpentine in its character in earlier history. After reminding the reader that the serpent in the garden of Eden is by the Christian world identified with Satan, while Moses' serpent was an emblem of Jehovah, so far at least as appertained to his omnipotent healing energies and divine guardianship—we will remark that other and older nations, or religions, than the Jews and Christians made use of the serpent as a mystical figure or representation of both good and evil personified that is, both the Deity and Devil; or, as some expressed it, he was both

creator and destroyer—creating himself anew, it
was thought, every time he threw off his old
exterior covering, and exhibited a new one, while
his venomous bite destroyed whomsoever made
battle with him. And the venom in the fangs of
the serpent being fatal, like that deadly moral
poison instilled into the souls of mortals by the
great adversary and arch-enemy of the human
race, while his (the serpent's) resistless fascinating powers being supposed to resemble the wily
insinuations and seductive allurements of the
"Evil One," aptly and powerfully hinted the
propriety of using the former to represent the
latter—in other words, the propriety of identify-
ing the Serpent and Satan together.

Hence the serpent became a Devil or *the
Devil*. Here then we have another example of the
same name being used in application to both God
and the Devil, evidencing still further the truth
of our proposition, that they were originally
comprehended in one being, as all the names and
titles of the Father, Son and Satan, which we
have thus far enumerated, most clearly indicate.
We have shown that the same names essentially,
and in some cases literally, were applied
indiscriminately to Jehovah, Jesus Christ and the
Devil, from which we must certainly readily infer
that they were originally considered one in
essence—that is, were derived from the same

imperfect perception, and consequently unitary conception of good and evil blended and confounded together.

This view of the case is corroborated by Christian testimony. The Rev. Mr. Pitrat (in his "Pagan Origin of Partialists' Doctrines," p. 58), quotes the Grecian poet, Euripides, as saying, "In no case is good separated from the evil. There must be a mixture of one and of the other." The author adds: "This opinion is of immemorial antiquity, and has been held by theologians, legislators, poets and philosophers."

Thus the opinion is indicated to have been of general prevalency as well as of great antiquity, that all good and evil (and of course, their personified representatives, God and Satan), were co-essentially, at least, inseparably one, as we have indicated to have been the belief of "God's holy people;" or to state the thing more definitely, the Jews, and their Pagan ancestors, if we recur to a very early date in human history, had no Devil, but comprehended all conceptions of good and evil in one being, so that when the perception of good and evil as distinct elements and characteristics began to be made, and a distinctive line drawn between them, and as a consequence a new author hunted up or conjured up for the latter, his names and titles were borrowed from that compound being, Jehovah, who had hitherto been regarded as the common source and creator of both good and evil. It was not until man's moral perceptions had so far matured as to fancy a distinct line of separation or demarkation between virtue and vice, that a Devil or personified evil genius was created in man's imagination, as the Father, Creator, or Author of the latter. And even at this period their perceptions, or appreciation of a distinction between moral and immoral actions, were so weak and imperfect, that the new-fangled or newly created author of the latter still passed for a God, deserving homage, and not entirely devoid of moral qualities. In fact, some nations regarded him but little inferior to God (that is, the first or original God), except with respect to power; and even Christians at this day concede him to be very nearly equal (if not in fact superior) in this respect, as he out-generals God Almighty, and captures nearly all his subjects, according to their own showing, and the teaching of their own Bible. So nearly equal at first was the great Evil Genius to the God of infinite goodness, that he was by some nations regarded as a twin-brother. We will quote history in proof:

"With regard to evil spirits," says an author, "the growth of ideas seems to have been very gradual. In the beginning, there was no distinct and defined separation between good and evil in the minds of men. In Hindoo theology, the same God destroyed and reproduced, and was not supposed to be impelled by wicked motives in his work of destruction any more than nature is. In Egypt the two powers were divided, but the malignant Typho was twin-brother of Osyrus the Good.

And it should be treasured in memory here, as will be observed from this quotation, that the first distinction or classification of good and evil did not appertain to moral actions of men, but was restricted entirely to the physical nature, the operations of the elements, etc. For a long period the attention of mankind seems to have been wholly directed to the phenomena of the physical external world, and for a long time they rested in the opinion that the same being, the same God who had created, also destroyed—the same being who sent down the genial solar rays of vernal spring, also sent the chilling, desolating blasts of winter; the same God who poured down the genial, gentle showers to revive the drooping flowers, the withered grass, and parched up dying cereals, also darted forth the forked lightning and blasting thunderbolt. But at length, as men's observations grew broader, and their perceptions became more distinct, their cogitations ripened into conviction or conclusion that there was too great a difference between the creative energies and desolating or destroying effects of Nature to be the product of one and the same being. And hence was originated the prime Evil Genius or Evil One, to stand as sponsor or author of the evil actions, not of men, but of Nature—not of the moral world, but the natural world.

"It is impossible," says the Grecian philosopher and historian, Plutarch, in his "Hermes," "that one sole being, either good or bad, can be the author of all, for God can cause no evil."

And hence he tells us on the next page: "We must admit two opposite causes, two contrary powers, leaning the one to the right and the other to the left. As the good can not produce evil, then there is a principle causing evil as well as as one causing good."

Thus reasoned the priest of Apollo and philosopher of Greece.

"We see by this passage," adds the Rev. Mr. Pitrat, "that the true origin of the two principles (God and Satan) proceeds from the difficulty which men in all times found in explaining by one sole cause, good and evil *in nature.*"

Besides the cases and examples which we have just submitted, we might refer to the theories of various ancient nations to show that the original conception of a Devil or evil genius was that of a God ruling over a portion of the empire of Nature, or what was generally considered the adverse antagonistic or evil portion of Nature. In the ancient Chaldeo-Persian system, he held dominion over all the aquatic portion of animals and birds. In other countries his empire was more restricted.

Speaking of the ancients in general, Plutarch says: "They believed in two Gods of different trades, if I may say so, who caused the one good and the other evil. They called the first, God, by excellence, and the second demon." Of the Persians, he says: "They believed that the first was of the nature of light, and the second that of darkness."

This accords exactly with the modern Christian theory.

"Among the Egyptians," he continues, "the first was called Osyrus, and the second Typhon, eternal foe to the first."

To show that the notion or doctrine of a personal evil agent, the author and embodiment of all evil, is not a tenet peculiar to Christianity, but is of very ancient Heathen origin, and prevailed very extensively in the world long before the era of Christianity, or advent of Christ, we will cite briefly a few other examples. Augustine tells us: "The ancient Assyrians, as well as the Persians, admitted two principles, whom they honored as two Gods, the one good, and the other bad."

The Rev. Mr. Pitrat says: "The inhabitants of Tologomy (India), believe that two principles govern the Universe, the one good, who is light, and the other bad, who is darkness."

He further says: "The Peruvians (of South America) revered Pacha-Carnac as being a good God, and Cupai as being a bad God. The Caribs admitted two sorts of spirits, one benevolent, who dwelt in Heaven and invited us to do good, the other evil who hovered over us to lead us into temptation. Those of Terra Firma think that there is a God in heaven—the sun. Besides, they admit a bad principle, who is the author of all evil."

The inhabitants of the kingdom of Pegu might be referred to as holding similar notions. Also the Portugese, who style the great evil genius, Demon. The Hottentots call the good principle "The Captain of Above," and the bad principle, "The Captain of Below." The latter is known as Touqua. The archdemon of the native of the island of Formosa is Chang, and their supreme God, Ishy. Among the inhabitants of the island of Teneriffe, the Devil is known by the name of Guyotta.

The people of Coterdea believe in two Gods— one white and good, the other black and evil. Among the Scandinavians, the evil God is known by the name of Locke, and is believed to make

perpetual war against the good God (Thor). In
Brazil, his Satanic Majesty passes by the name of
Aguyan, while among the Tartars of Katzchenzi
he is known as Tous. The Devil of the Manicheans is Hyle. The Esquimaux, says the Rev.
Mr. Pitrat, believe in a God supremely good,
whom they call Ukouna, and in another Ouikan,
who is the author of all evils, who causes the
tempests and who capsizes the boats—verse 63.
He says also, "The Siamese sacrifice to an evil
spirit whom they consider as being the cause of
all the misfortunes of mankind," which is similar
to the idea of the Hottentots, who say that, "From
him all evils flow to this world." I will add here
that the Chaldeans had their evil stars (as well
as good ones), which they believed were controlled
by a Devil or evil spirits. And thus says Plutarch,
"The dogma of two principles (two Gods) was
admitted by nearly all nations." Thus we
perceive that the most ancient notions of a Devil
or Evil Genius was, First, That of a being
antagonistic to God, and yet himself a God, the
two possessing many similar characteristics and
on nearly an equal footing with respect to power
and jurisdiction, being in Persia "own brothers,"
twins. Second, The sphere of his operations was
at first restricted in most theogonies to physical
nature. Third, He was graciously devised to
save God from the stigma of being considered the

author of evil, a logical deduction from the premises that a good and pure being could not be the same, or author of that which was not good—or anything evil. A further research into the great arcana of Nature would have taught them that all evil, both moral and physical, is simply a natural concomitant of the crude germinal immature state of nature, which will disappear as the world matures and ripens into perfection. Fourth, It will be observed, that nothing is said about the smoking pit or infernal regions, as it had not at that time been discovered or thought of. A Columbus had not as yet sailed in that direction. The respective thrones of the two omnipotent Gods was situated in the stars or among the elements. The good God some placed in the sun, while his rival antagonist was consigned to the moon or some of the planets, as all theological conceptions at that period were connected with the starry heavens, more or less. The distance of the two kingdoms apart is not known. In Persia, they were situated so near together that Mithra the Mediator, or, as Plutarch calls him, the Inter-Mediator, being situated between them, could transmit messages from one to the other, and interfered or intermediated to settle their difficulties and disputes, from which circumstance he received the name of Mediator. It will be recollected that the two kingdoms in the Christian system were situated so near together that Dives and Lazarus, or Dives and Abraham conversed together, though it must have required hallooing on the highest key to be heard across the "impassable gulf" situated between them.

That the Devil, Satan, or "the Old Serpent," was at first a co-equal God, and not invested with the odious repulsive character with which we now find him represented by the Christian world, we find further evidence of in the ancient diagrams used in physical astronomy. By examining the astronomical charts, maps, and textbooks used in our schools and colleges, it will be found that the Serpent is pictured under the twofold aspect or character of "A Good God," and "An Evil God." In the first place, we find him represented under the name of "The Hydra," extending through and including three constellations, that of the Crab, the Lion and the Virgin, thus representing the three summer months, June, July and August. And then we find another diagram of the Serpent in another part of the heavens under the name of "The Scorpion," beginning the winter season— inaugurating the dreaded inauspicious October, the harbinger of cold and dreary evil Winter. And thus he was used to represent or symbolize both good and evil; which, when personified, were God and the Demon. We can easily understand, therefore, why Moses and the Israelites, as well as the Egyptians and Hindoos, had both a good Serpent and an evil Serpent—the latter figuring in Eden, the former constructed of brass and displayed on a pole. And the statement or theological proposition, that the Great Emperor, "Charge d'Affairs" of the smoky regions was once considered a God, is still further confirmed by the fact that he was formerly in several religions a co-equal member of the Trinity, "hail fellow well met" in the triads of Gods. The third member of the Trinity in India, Egypt, Persia, and I believe Mexico, also, was a representation and personification of evil in their most ancient legends, which furnishes evidence indisputable, that they stood in the relation and occupied the position of Gods. We may legitimately conceive that although the character of the two at first stood nearly parallel with respect to moral attributes, yet as time rolled on and developed and matured the moral perception of the people and capacitated them to demark or discriminate good and evil, they would, in imagination, see the two Gods diverging morally wider and wider apart and becoming more and more hostile to each other, until finally they would become, and did become, directly, antipodes, and in deadly array, strife, and opposition to each other in nearly every conceivable respect, though in all the change the Evil God did not lose his power or sway. He still retained almost uncurtailed omnipotent power with which he was at first invested, though his tenure or jurisdiction was gradually removed from the physical or natural to the moral world, so that the seat of his empire is now in the minds of men, and not among the physical elements or planets as formerly. Such has been the work of man's imagination.

CHAPTER VII

ORIGIN OF THE TERMS ''KINGDOM OF HEAVEN,''
''GATES OF HELL,'' ALSO OF TRADITIONS OF THE
DRAGON CHASING THE WOMAN, THE WOMAN
CLOTHED WITH THE SUN, ETC.

The Christian theory, as we have briefly
stated on a previous occasion, so far from
restricting the power or empire of the Evil One,
grants him the lion's share, allowing him to carry
off the major portion of the human family,
having first permitted him to construct a broad
guage or ''broad road'' for the purpose, and
''many there be who go in thereat,'' while they
have the road leading to the other kingdom so
very narrow that ''few there be who find it.''
And thus they permit ''the Prince of Darkness''
to carry off to his subterranean empire nearly
the whole retinue of souls which God had created
for the purpose of his own glory, and thus
thwart the main object of creation. We observe,
from the authorities quoted, that the perception
of physical evil, or natural evil, preceded that
of the perception and recognition of moral
evil; and that the physical evils first recognized,
were those produced by the violence of the

70

elements and the rotation of the seasons. Winter was, with her cold bleak drapery and her widespread desolation and destruction, in the estimation or imagination of the ancients, the principle and most prolific source of evil—*i.e.,* the God of Winter. The principal inhabitants of the earth, as heretofore intimated, having noticed that during six months of the year the powers at work in Nature were engaged in fructifying, vivifying, beautifying, producing, etc., and that during the other six months some apparently adverse power arrested, blasted, and destroyed those desirable operations and their results, they hence imagined two contrary hostile powers, engaged in perpetual war against each other; and as the six Spring and Summer months were attended with almost perpetual sunshine, and the growth and production of fruits and flowers, and culinary or edible vegetables, things that were calculated to supply their natural wants, they were regarded as constituting, and became known as "the true kingdom," or "kingdom of Heaven," while the winter months were denominated "the kingdom of Darkness."

The former was also called "the kingdom of the Sun," or God who dwelt in the sun. This imaginary entrance to the kingdom, which it was supposed opened to the sun as he left the tropic of Cancer to travel back to the South, was called "the gates of Heaven," while the fancied passage through the other tropics constituted "the gates of Hell." At the first stood the Lamb, the zodiacal sign of Spring, to usher in the glorious sun, or sun-God, as he drove up with his fiery steed to the portals of Paradise in early Spring. At the latter, stood the hideous Scorpion, Dragon, or Devil, ready to drag everything accessible to his clutches or power, down into his bottomless pit, at one time hitching his tail over and pulling down one-third of the stars. Hence you will discover, that the Devil is from above, and not from below, though he descends below every six months into Hades, as hereafter explained. You will find by consulting your almanacs, that Aries, the Lamb or Ram, is the zodiacal or astronomical sign for March, the first Spring month. And the Scorpion was (though the Eagle is now) the sign of October, first Winter month (in the bisectional division of the year); that is, by dividing the year into two seasons of six months each. St. John (Rev. xii) speaks of the Dragon having power to hurt the five months, and astronomically speaking, he does hurt the vegetable productions of the five principal prolific months of the year, with a vengeance. And St. John's monster, with the seven heads and ten horns, may find a solution in astronomy, or astrotheology, by assuming the seven heads to be the seven Summer months (as

some nations divided the year in this way), and
duplicating the five Winter months for the horns.
And then, the story of the Dragon "pursuing the
woman to destroy her male child," finds an easy
explanation here. Turn to your almanacs, and
you will notice that the Dragon or Scorpion is in
pursuit of the woman, Virgin, sure enough, being
the next sign in order in the zodiac; or direct your
eyes to the heavens in a cloudless night, you will
observe that just after the old maid (a virgin with
a child in her arms, as the Persians show her)
rises above the horizon in the East, up comes the
old Scorpion called a serpent among the Persians;
a Dragon in Phœnicia; Draco among the Romans,
which is the Latin for Dragon. Virgil calls him
Maximus Angis, the Great Snake. (See Georgius
8). The great Dragon, according to astronomical
diagrams, is actually after the woman (Virgin)
and her child, and was for thousands of years
B.C., and until modern astronomers caught him,
and cast him into the bottomless pit, and substi-
tuted the eagle in his place.

How easy it is to imagine, when, by observing
in the almanac, that the Dragon or Scorpion (the
same thing) is the next sign after the Virgin,
that he is chasing her through the sky! And it
may be more than fancy to associate the woman
and Serpent here with the scene in Eden, wherein
a serpent is represented as tempting a woman

(Mother Eve) to masticate a pippin with her new incisors and molars, which never before had been used. And as we find a man also (Aquarius) among the signs of the zodiac, this may be Father Adam; for it is more agreeable, not to say honorable, to fancy or conceive of our first parents being formed among the stars, than in a mud-hole, according "As the Lord said unto Moses." The prophet Daniel speaks of a great contest between a ram and a goat (see chapter iv), and both of these you will find represented in our zodiac and apparently (to a fanciful imagination) chasing each other through the heavens. And again, St. John's marvelous figure of "a woman clothed with the sun, the moon under her feet and a crown of twelve stars upon her head" (Rev. xii), is easily understood when viewed through an astronomical mirror. More appropriately may the astronomical virgin woman be said to be clothed with the sun, than could be said of any other of the twelve signs of the zodiac, judging from her situation among the signs and her relative position to the sun. There she stands, right in the focus of the sun's rays in August, the hottest month in the year, and thus is clothed with the sun more brilliantly than that of any other sign. Of course the moon is under her feet, while the twelve months of the year, or the twelve signs of the zodiac form her crown of twelve stars. Now mark! we are not becoming "wise above what is written," for these things are all written, not merely in your school-books, but in your almanacs, copied' from the skies.

The sun's crossing the equinoctial line in March, was an event of great moment to some of the ancient nations, as it ushered in the thousand blessings of Spring and Summer. We cannot wonder, therefore, that the cross became a sacred emblem in nearly all the religions of the earth. Now let it be noted here, that the scenes which I have depicted as occurring in the starry heavens are not mere fanciful pictures of my own conjuring up, but are matters of actual record in the histories or sacred books of Persia, Egypt, India and Rome. Take for example the story, or allegory, of a woman pursued by a Dragon, Serpent or Devil, etc., (all one according to St. John, the Revelator and mystigogue); this is not only found substantially related in several mythological histories, but was in Persia represented on the celestial globes. And Kircher, Seldon, Eben, Manobius, and Scaliger, (Note ad Manil, p. 341), furnish evidence of its being referred to in astronomical works of several nations.

It will be recollected that St. John describes the woman as being clothed with the sun and chased by a Dragon or Serpent (for both terms are used, see Revelations xii), which seeks to devour her child, and pours out a flood of water after her as she flees into the wilderness to save her child. In the Grecian version of the story Latona, being about to be confined, flies into a desert isle to save her child from Python, the Serpent or Dragon; while the Persians, according to Scaliger, had the virgin woman represented on their astronomical globes or planispheres with a child in her arms, holding two "ears of corn" (wheat) in her hand, and with wings spread in the act of flying from her pursuer, as represented by St. John and the Eygptian version of the same story. And the child of this virgin in the Persian legend was born on the 25th of December, and it has been long since the people of that country first celebrated the 25th of December as the birthday of Oxus the Savior and child of this virgin. The pursuer spoken of in this story is with the Persians, Ahrimanes, the God of darkness, and is the Typhon of the Egyptians, the Lucifer of the Greeks, the Python of the Romans, the Obi of the Africans, the Manitou of the American Indians, the Dragon of St. John, and the Serpent or Dragon of the North Pole. And he actually begins to raise his head above the horizon, according to Burritt's "Geography of the Heavens," immediately after the rising of the virgin—the sign in the zodiac for August. The Egyptian version fills out the scene and represents the river Orion in the act of pouring out its waters just as the virgin appears above the horizon, which is the river St. John tells us the Dragon poured out after the woman and her child, to drown and wash them away.

Now all these figures are represented in Burritt's Astronomy, used in all our schools. Plutarch tells us that the Egyptians painted their Serpents or Dragons red, which reminds us of St. John's language, "The great red Dragon." (See Revelations xii). Theon says there is no sign in the zodiac on which so much fable has been founded as that of the virgin. The ancients, including several nations (Persia, India, etc.), chose the figure of the virgin to represent the fruitfulness of the earth; and as the sun commenced rising at the 25th of December toward Spring, the season of fruitfulness and plenty, it was said, therefore, figuratively, to bring forth a new-born child. Now, as it can be shown, and is conceded, that the Pagan version of this is older than the Christian version, we may venture to suggest that St. John was not the author of the first edition of it.

CHAPTER VIII

Strange as it may seem, it is nevertheless true, that even the Christian fabled Hell may be found (like most others of their venerated and Pagan-derived myths and mysteries) among the stars, though they generally point the other way, or in the other direction, when they wish to indicate its locality, not reflecting that Dives and Lazarus would not have conversed together while one was in Heaven and the other in Hell, unless these two places had occupied contiguous localities—at least, been situated near together, and this was as likely above as below. The word astronomers use to indicate the sun in its highest point of ascension is perihelion. Now you may notice there is a Hell in this word (peri-*hel*-ion): at least it can be traced to Hell, or Hell to it. *Hel*ion, the last part of this word, was pronounced by the Greeks *Elios,* and is synonymous with Acheron, which is generally translated Hell. So that we have "peri," which means around, about, and "helion," *Hell*—that is, the sun roundabout Hell. We can not think it strange, therefore, that Hell

78

is a pretty warm place. And let me admonish the reader not to be alarmed if we should find good old Elias in Hell, the same who appeared with Moses at Christ's transfiguration. For it is a fact that Elias (the Greeks using the aspirate instead of the *H*) is about synonymous, as I have already stated, with the Greek Acheron, which is rendered Hell by translators. Hence it follows that Elias means Hell, if not Hell-fire, which will account for his face shining with such lustre at the transfiguration.

And Hades, or Ades (for the Greek alphabet has no *H*) may be traced with still less difficulty to the sun for its origin. And Ades, it is well-known, frequently occurs in the Greek New Testament for Hell, and is so rendered in English. Well, now, Ades analyzed is *Ad,* an Ammorian name for God or God-sun, and *es* the fire; and *hence* means "the God-fire," "sun-fire." It was the belief of some of the ancient nations (the Greeks, for instance) that Heaven and Hell were nearly contiguous, being separated only by an impassable gulf, and both, as some believe, are located in the sun, though more generally the former only was located there.

CHAPTER IX

The "bottomless pit" had a different origin from that of Hades, or Hell. Its geographical position was a fancied one beyond the South Pole. This location grew out of the persuasion of some of the ancients, that their dreaded and devastating winters came from that quarter, and hence "the Evil God, who produced the winters (known as "Winter God"), had his seat of empire there. A circumstance which facilitated or contributed to this superstition was that of its being beyond the purview or reach of the natural vision. And as it was apparently situated below them, and they could not conceive of its having any bottom, they hence called it the "bottomless pit." Winter was supposed to come from the South, because it was observed to come upon them as the sun receded southward, which some imagined had some agency in sending the winter. And the sun going down below the horizon out of sight in the Arctic regions so as to result in darkness, was supposed or fancied to die, but it was born again or arose from the dead when it reappeared in Spring or arose again above the horizon. And as it approached the "gates of Spring," "the Lamb of God," or the Lamb of March gathered up "the sins of the world," or the sins of the Winter, and bore them away. And thus was realized, astronomically, not only "the Lamb of God taking away the sins of the world," but also the death and resurrection of the Son of God, or the sun-God, more properly. While the South Pole was the great "bottomless pit," the fancied abode of demons and devils, and also the synonym of everything evil, the North Pole as the supposed residence of "the Good God," was called "the Mountain of the Lord"—as nearly every nation had its "Mountain of the Lord" or "Holy Mountain."

CHAPTER X

The fact has been disclosed by the foregoing
historical exegesis or sketch of Satanic biography
that the capers and diabolical operations of the
Devils, Demons and evil genii of the Oriental
nations, were at first confined to the skies or
starry heavens. But it is important to observe
that in the course of time their sphere of
operations was transferred to the earth, and
finally to "the underground world" beneath the
earth, long prior to the dawn of the Christian
era. According to the mythological era
of Oriental Egypt, when the Great Dragon,
Serpent, or Devil, Python or Typhon was
conquered by the archangel of Apollo, and hurled
down headlong from the battlements of Heaven
(and thus became a fallen angel), he was thrown,
body, hoofs and horns into lake Sibon, or Sirbonis,
situated at the foot of Mount Casius. This lake
was chosen as the place of consignment for the
great Arch-Demon or Arch-Enemy of the human
race, because it had become a haunt for the most
weird and wild imagination, and a focus for the

82

most disagreeable and detestable association of ideas that ever nestled in the brain of a superstitious people. Hence it became universally execrated. Bearing these facts in mind, let us observe that when the Nile overflowed its banks, as it did semi-annually, and spread over the country for many miles around, it reached this lake Sirbonis, and submerged it with its putrid waters. And, as it receded into its channel by the subsidence of the current, it deposited in the lake a great amount of debris, putrefying vegetation, and nauseating substances of various kinds. And it is a matter of fact or fable, that upon its stagnant waters, there accumulated a scum bearing a strong analogy in taste, color and smell, to that of brimstone or sulphur. In fact, some authors speak of it as being veritably and truly brimstone in solution—*i.e.,* sulphur. Travelers and historians tell us that when the sun shone upon this brilliant mirror-like floating substance, it presented the appearance of being on fire, and from that circumstance was called "the lake of fire and brimstone," while the steam, gas, vapor or miasma created and eliminated by the action of the sun upon the deposits of mud and slime around the margin of the lake, ascending upward, formed the imaginary smoke of the imaginary place (as it is fabled to be) of endless torment, which from time immemorial has been the source of fear, fable and fiction, to the ignorant, credulous and superstitious people of various countries, and which now causes the pious Christian to "work out his salvation with fear and trembling." This lake being situated in a warm climate, became the habitation of various kinds of aquatic or amphibious monsters and noxious vermin, which the imagination and credulity of an age of superstitious fear could easily transform into "imps of darkness," or evil genii and frightful hobgoblins, while the hideous noises issuing unceasingly from the mouths of the numerous denizens of this "frightful waste of waters," augmented and heightened by the glare of the host of Jack-'o-lanterns, Will-'o-wisps, and other nocturnal lights pecular to the moist or humid atmosphere of warm climates, finished the imaginary picture of a Demon's home and a Devil's Hell. And as the inundation of the river, together with the overflow of the lake, often produced a great amount of damage, destroying cattle and other domestic animals, dwellings, etc., it was very easy and very natural for the childish superstition which held supreme sway three thousand five hundred years ago, to believe that the great giant foe of human bliss and human beatitude, the imaginary Typhon had something to do in producing these calamitous and direful events; more especially as it was assumed as an axiom indisputable, that the "righteous Apollo, the God of the skies," was too transcendantly good, too merciful and too benignant to his creatures, to have any agency in such business. And here it may be mentioned that it was currently reported that human beings residing in the vicinity of the lake were occasionally borne away in the clutches of the hydra-headed Typhon "to parts unknown," to be disposed of in accordance with his diabolical designs and infernal purposes, and that the smell of brimstone encountered upon their receding pathway, disclosed unmistakably the damnable fate of these luckless human victims. This tradition brings to mind the story of the Hibernian who, while in America hearing the funeral of a priest spoken of, remarked, "we do not go to the trouble of burying priests and pickpockets in our country." "What do you do with them when they die?" inquired a bystander. "Well, when they give up the ghost, we lay out the defunct bodies in an open room, and the next morning they are gone, and nothing more is observable but a strong scent of brimstone in the room, and the mark of diabolical footsteps on the floor. This is all we know about the matter."

We have, then, fully disclosed in the foregoing sketch of Satanic history the origin of the tradition, nearly four thousand years old, of a "lake of fire and brimstone," with its imaginary

potentate—it being originally nothing more or
less than lake Sirbonis with its fancy hatched
ruler, the redoubtable long-tailed, double-headed
Typhon. "He who hath ears to hear let him
hear," and no longer tremble with fear when he
encounters the smell of brimstone. The tradition
respecting "The worm that never dies" (Mark ix:
44), had its origin likewise in Egypt, and started
from the circumstance of a gnawing, stinging
worm which infests that country (a fire-eater
by tradition), being never known to die, simply
because, as later researches show, it burrows down
into the soil before it dies; hence, not being seen
after its death, it was supposed to be immortal.
It was found within the precincts of the "fiery
lake," and was supposed to be one of the infernal
agents in the employ of his Satanic Majesty, the
horny, iron-hoofed Typhon.

CHAPTER XI

St. John tells us (see Rev. xxi: 10) he saw the
New Jerusalem descend from God out of Heaven,
and as we have shown by previous historical
disclosures in this work, that Hell also descended
from above; it being a much older institution than
the New Jerusalem, we suggest the propriety of
styling it "the Old Jerusalem." We have followed
it in its descent to the earth. We will now trace
it to its present locality, "the under-ground
world," whither it was removed several thousand
years ago. Various and multifarious were the
notions among the ancients with respect to the
substantial whereabouts of the fabled Hell—the
after-death depository for wicked souls. Some
fancied its location in the sun, others referred
its geographical position to the moon; others
again imagined its unquenchable fires raged in the
bowels of the earth, but the opinion finally became
somewhat prevalent that it was hung or planted
under the earth. Mr. Higgins' remarks relative
to the ancient tradition with respect to its locality,
that "the lower or southern hemisphere which is

hid in darkness in winter, and which is always
attended with darkness, decay, disease and death,
and every kind of discomfort, became imaginarily
controlled by, and consequently the abode of evil
beings, now known as demons, devils, etc., and the
abode itself as Hell, while the upper hemisphere
was the abode of celestial beings, as gods, angels,
etc." And no less various were the notions with
respect to its character, than with respect to its
locality. Mr. Higgins shows that many believed
it to be a place of "utter darkness," and a very
cold place. This was perhaps before its combustible faggots had been lighted up or set on fire.
The name for Hell among the ancient Celts was
Ilfin, which means "cold climate," which shows
that they also regarded it as a cold country. The
ancient Gauls and Britons, Goths and Germans,
taught that Hell was a place of "dreadful darkness," and was infested with venomous reptiles,
ferocious beasts and wicked spirits. The
Egyptian astrologers taught that Hell was a
"bottomless pit," the damned inmates being
suspended on hooks fixed in the side of the pit,
though many of the natives of that country held
to a "lake of fire and brimstone." The ancient
Buddhist and Mexicans believed in a Hell of
"unquenchable fire prepared for the Devil and his
angels." Here it may be remarked that the
inhabitants of cold countries taught that Hell was

a hot place—a place of "glowing, melting heat," while on the other hand, the inhabitants of warm climates taught that the place of consignment for the wicked was "as cold as a mountain of ice." So that all who were captured and carried away to Pluto's realms by old "Plug Ugly," underwent a change of climate, whether they hailed from the torrid or frigid zone.

CHAPTER XII

Here we wish it distinctly noted as an important historical fact, that the conception of a Devil and a Hell long existed before the remotest idea was entertained that either had anything to do with or any connection with punishment in a future life. Both had a fabled existence in the external world among the physical elements long before the Devil was made an *agent* of punishment, or Hell a *place* of punishment for the wicked after death in the imaginations of the people. Indeed, we are credibly informed, the Manicheans long believed Hell to be the blissful abode of the righteous. The first conception of evil and malevolent beings, as we have just intimated, restricted their sphere of operations to the physical world, to the violent storms and destructive elements, and all the unpropitious events of nature. In their utter ignorance of natural causes, a superstitious age would naturally assign such things to imaginary beings. But no thought seems to have been entertained, that the malicious denizens of the "evil world" had anything to do with the thoughts or actions of men—not even the most wicked and vicious; for the reason that man's moral perceptions were not at that period sufficiently developed to observe any distinction between good and bad actions. The nature and effects of immoral actions had not been as yet discovered; everything, as in the Jewish Bible, was ascribed to God. Their perception of any distinction or line of demarkation between virtue and vice ran too low (if they possessed any) to incite even the thought that any action or line of conduct that any man could pursue, could be sufficiently bad or criminal to require any punishment to be sent after him, and inflicted on him after he left this world. Nor had the priesthood as yet acquired sufficient ascendency over the people to lead them to invent a Hell to punish delinquent pew-renters or tithe payers, as we shall hereafter show it to be an institution of their getting up. As man's moral perceptions grew and expanded and ripened into the conviction that some actions were good and some bad to such a degree of difference as to require a separate and distinct source for their origin, he began to look around him to find a way of accounting for each class of actions separately. And as the heavens above and the great imaginary abyss below the earth were already peopled with imaginary beings of different and opposite characters, it was easy—it was natural to begin to associate these beings with the actions of men, and to conclude that all good actions were incited by good beings or by "the good God," as they styled the Supreme Being,and all evil and immoral actions by the "evil God," "the master mischief-maker." And the conception in this respect seems to have been at first wholly anthropomorphic and unspiritual, or sensuous—at least local and circumscribed. The Devil, it was thought, could not influence the actions of men unless bodily present with them. He was not then, as now, omnipresent, and invested with the omnipotent power to tempt or seduce millions at a time, though scattered all over the globe at an immeasurable distance both from him and from each other. The Hindoos, Buddhists, Burmese, and some of the Chinese taught that the maleficent beings called devils or demons entered body, head and heels, into the minds of men, and from there rolled out their evil thoughts and prompted them to vicious actions. Most of the ancient religious teachers of the Oriental schools taught that "old king Satan" was supplied with a numerous train or retinue of inferior sub-devils, who acted as sub-agents in the work of decoying souls and leading them into perdition. The

Hindoo Bible (the Shaster), more than three thousand years old, teaches this doctrine, and tells us that the demi-devils (or Devs, as it styles them, lacking but one syllable of making the Christian's Devil), were completely under the control of the master demon or devil-in-chief, and entered the minds of men at his bidding; but that they could be ejected at any time by exorcisms and prayers of the priests, especially if the patients' pockets were well lined with "filthy lucre," which often seemed to operate as a powerful charm in the way of dispelling the diabolical intruders from "the inner man," and henceforth keeping them at a respectable distance.

Now, the foregoing notions of the Orientalists seem to be fully recognized and acknowledged by Christ and his Apostles as a part of the Christian "plan of salvation." No less than nine times is Christ represented as "casting out devils," and on several occasions as having a familiar chat with them. At one time he is said to have ousted seven at a clip. They were tumbled *nolens volens,* pell mell, out of a respectable Christian lady whom we would naturally have supposed was too high-minded to entertain such "low company."

CHAPTER XIII

THE CHRISTIAN'S DEVIL—WHENCE IMPORTED OR
BORROWED

We have stated, in a previous chapter, that
the primitive Jews did not teach the doctrine of
future endless punishment—they evidently knew
nothing of the doctrine until after their exile to
Babylon, as we do not find the doctrine taught in
any of their writings penned previous to that era.
The first traces of it are found in the "lesser"
or later prophets, now termed Apocryphal, and
the Talmuds, or Mischna, written but a few
centuries prior to the Christian era. And from
these sources, in all probability, the founders of
the Christian religion derived, in part, their doctrines and traditions on this subject. Though we
find the after-death primitive doctrines of the New
Testament are an admixture of Babylonian or
Chaldaic, Egyptian and Syrian traditions on this
subject, and all conform approximately to the still
more ancient Buddhists' doctrine of future
rewards and punishments. The Egyptian Devil
was a huge monster, panoplied with horns, and
"shod" with hoofs, a formidable tail of unmem-
tionable, if not immeasurable length, which we

suppose served as a kind of rudder as he "flew his giddy rounds amongst the sons and daughters of men," though it appears he doffed his tail for the convenience of inserting his legs into a pair of breeches, that he might join the respectable society which he accompanied as they went to attend a picnic at the house of Job, in Chaldea. We frequently hear instances spoken of "of a descent from the sublime to the ridiculous;" but here is a case of the *ascent* from the ridiculous to the sublime, presented in the account of Satan's becoming a "hail fellow well met" with the sons of God, as they journeyed to make an important negotiation with that "servant of the Lord," Job. He must have felt honored and exalted in the highest degree by such a peculiar favor being vouchsafed to his majesty.

We have stated in effect that the founders of the Christian religion (perhaps while yet Jews) obtained their model for a Devil from the Babylonians during their bondage in the country. It is well to remark, however, that Christians have invested his long-tailed majesty also with some of the characteristics of the Egyptian Devil, as we find in the illustrated works of the early Christians he is represented with horns, hoofs, and a rear appendage of lawless dimensions. We will conclude our answer to the question, "Where did the Christian world obtain their Devil?" by presenting an extract from an able writer on the subject, who tells us "The ancient Egyptians had a Devil called Typhon, afterward engrafted into the Greek mythology, as the author of Evil. The later Jews, who became followers of Christ and the founders of the Christian system, admired the idea of having such a fearful ugly Devil (as he had horns, hoofs and a tail), and hence engrafted his monstrous physical proportions on to the idea of a Devil they had obtained in Babylon. At the same time they gave him the malignant and ferocious character of Beelzebub, the Devil of Syria." And thus the question is explicitly answered.

CHAPTER XIV

It only now remains to be shown that the writers of the Christian New Testament must have copied from the ancient Pagans, as they have all their variously modified forms or modes of future endless *post mortem* punishment. In fact, the whole train of ideas and doctrines, apparently, both of a Devil and Hell, which we find incorporated in the Christian Scriptures as a part, seemingly, of the Gospel plan of salvation, are found likewise in the Pagan systems of mythology long antedating the inception of the, Christian religion. The Bible of the Christian speaks of—

A Hell of darkness (Matt. viii: 22, and Jude xii); a Hell of light—at least of fire, which must emit light (Matt. v: 22); a Hell in which both body and soul are destroyed (Matt. x: 28); a Hell in which the soul is eternally punished (Matt. xxv: 46); a limited Hell (Rev. xx: 13, and 2d Peter ii: 4); an endless Hell (Matt. xviii: 8); an upper (impliedly) and a lower Hell (Psalms lxxxvi: 13); a Hell, or lake of fire and brimstone (Rev. xiv: 10); a bottomless Hell or pit (Rev.

ix: 1); the keys of Hell (Rev. xx: 1); the chains of Hell, or the chains in Hell (2d Peter ii: 4); the Gates of Hell, etc. (Matt. xvi: 18).

Now, an examination of Mythological history will show that these ideas or conceptions, are of Pagan origin, together with the various Scripture notions and myths appertaining to a Devil or devils, such as:—

His being the author of evil; his leading or destroying or punishing them; his taking up his abode in the minds or souls of men, with his troop or train of inferior second class Devils or evil spirits; the saviors and saints casting them out of the temples of the "inner man;" their change of residence from the souls of men to the souls and stomachs of swine and other animals; also, the various metamorphoses or changes of the Devil-in-Chief, by which he sometimes appears as a crawling or creeping serpent; then as a roaring lion; at other times as a flying dragon; and occasionally as an "angel of light," etc., etc.

Some of these notions or conceptions have already been traced to Pagan origin. The origin of others will be indicated as we proceed to speak of the several Pagan doctrines or myths appertaining to future endless punishment, as compared with those found in the Christian Scriptures.

The Rev. Mr. Pitrat, in his work before mentioned, tells us, (p. 177):

"The Pagans believed that in their Hell there were two principal abodes (an upper and a lower Hell), the one expiatory, in which the common wicked were detained and tortured until they had expiated their faults, and been purified enough to be admitted into the Elysium (Heaven) and the other the filthiest, the darkest, and the deepest cavern, where great criminals were burnt and excruciated endlessly, and without any ,hope, cessation or relief in their torments."

The same author adds:

"According to Plato (400 B.C.), the dead who have been guilty of murder, sacrilege, and other enormous crimes, shall be endlessly miserable in Tartarus (Hell). Those whose crimes have not been so great, shall be detained therein for a year" (p. 211).

In the above extracts we have the Christian Bible doctrine of an "upper and a lower Hell," a "purgatory," an "endless Hell," "a fiery Hell," etc. Again, our author says:

"The Pagans believed that there was a gate to their Hell, at which (in Roman mythology) the frightful Tissiphon watched day and night, 'seeking whom he might devour,' and that Lucifer held the keys of the gates of Hell" (p. 175).

Here are disclosed several other Christian ideas of Hell:

"The Pagans believed that the deepest darkness reigned in their Hell" (p. 178).

Here is the Christian's Hell of "outer darkness." Speaking of Tartarus, our author says:

"There are incessantly heard the rattle of chains dragged by wretched victims, their groans, and the strokes of the lashes that tear their flesh" (p. 134).

Here are the chains spoken of in II Peter ii: 4. The Hindoo Vedas (written before Moses, according to Mr. Dow) informs us that:

"Yama (the judge, or "judge of quick and dead") delivers over the trembling wicked souls to evil spirits, in order to expose them to be lacerated by demons, or gnawed by fiery worms, or plunged into pits of flame."

Here we have presented "the bottomless pit," where "the worm dieth not, and the fire is not quenched." We might continue to trace out the parallel in every minute particular. But to present a full history or description of the numerous doctrines, notions, conceptions or myths, of the ancient superstitious Pagans relative to the after-death punishment of the wicked in Hell, Hades, Tartarus, Infernus, Gehenna, Tophet, Sheol, or the Fiery Pit, with the various operations and machinations of

Devils, Demons, Dragons, Serpents, Satans, Furies, Evil Spirits, or Wicked Genii, which were in vogue, and currently believed in thousands of years ago, when the deepest, darkest, and direst superstitions enveloped the human mind—a considerable portion of which we find copied into or rehearsed in the Christian Scriptures—such an exposition would require a large volume. We will conclude this branch of our subject by two quotations from different poets, one Pagan, and the other Christian, and observe the similitude of their train of ideas in attempting to depict the underground world.   Hear the poet Virgil, 60 B.C:

> "At Hell's dread mouth a thousand monsters wait,
> Grief weeps and vengeance bellows in the gate:
> Fierce, formidable fiends the portals keep,
> With pain, death, and death's half-brother, sleep.
> Here stretched on iron beds the furies roar,
> And close by, Lerna's hissing monster stands,
> Briarens, * * * * and all around
> Fierce harpies scream and direful gorgons frowned;
> Here rolls the roaring, flaming tide of Hell,
> And thundering rocks the fiery torrents swell."

Now let us observe how successfully the Christian Pollock has taken lessons in the Pagan school of infernal ideas, and how exactly he makes the Christian theory of Hell accord with that of the ancient heathen:

> "Beneath I saw a lake of burning fire,
> Tossing with tides of dark tempestuous wrath,
> And now wild shouts and wailing dire,

And shrieking infants swell the dreadful choir.
Here sits in bloody robes the fury fell,
By night and day to watch the gates of Hell.
Here you begin terrific groans to hear,
And sounding lashes rise upon the ear.
On every side the damned their fetters grate,
And curse 'mid clanking chains their wretched fate."

I leave the reader to compare the effusions of the ancient heathen bard with those of the Christian, two thousand years later, and to determine for himself which is the most Paganish or fiendish. The proposition which sustains or maintains the striking resemblance in the *post mortem* punishment theory of the ancient heathen nations and those of the Christian Bible, written at a later period, is sustained by even Christian writers, of which we will present one proof. The well-known popular (English) Christian clergyman, Mr. McKnight, in speaking of Christ's parable of the rich man and Lazarus, says:

"It must be acknowledged that our Lord's descriptions are not drawn from the writings of the Old Testament, but have a remarkable affinity to the description which the Grecian poets have given. They, as well as our Lord, represent the abodes of the blessed as lying contiguous to the regions of the damned, and separated only by a great impassable river, or deep gulf situated in such a condition that the ghosts could talk from one to another from its opposite banks. The parable says the souls of wicked men are tormented in flames. The Grecian mythologist tells us they lie in Plegethon, the river of fire, where they suffered torments.''

''He who hath ears to hear let him hear'' how a Christian divine thus affirms to the truth of our proposition, that the Christian's Hell is a transcript from Pagan tradition of heathen mythology.

CHAPTER XV

The conception of future punishment, or rather the thought of turning it to practical account in the way of influencing the actions and conduct of men, seems to have been first suggested to the officiating priests of ancient Egypt by the peculiar circumstances attending their mode of interring the dead. We are told that a certain cemetery belonging to one of the principal cities of Egypt, being situated at a considerable distance from the town, required the river Styx to be crossed in order to reach it; and before it could be crossed, the ferryman (Charon) must be satisfied by the payment of his fee. But in numerous cases the surviving relatives were too poor to raise it, and the fee had to be paid by the public, or if not thus paid, the body of the defunct was thrown into the ditch to be devoured by dogs and vermin, or cast into the river Acheron, which means Hell—at least Christian writers so interpret and translate it. Thus, this river was made the receptacle of the bodies of those who, on account of their vices, were excluded (so the multitude were taught) from the common obsequies of the dead and the favors of Heaven, or rather its Supreme Ruler Jove, while the righteous, if poor, were always honored with a decent burial at the public expense. To decide whether the defunct had led a life sufficiently virtuous to deserve an honorable interment, men were chosen, called "Episcopes," from the Greek *epi* (over) and *skopeo*, to see or look and thus literally means to see over or oversee. And thus originated the term and the sacradotal for Episcopacy now found in the Methodist and other churches. For the accommodation of the instituted order of priesthood, towers or buildings were erected which are now known as temples and churches. And this dates the origin of the priesthood and their officiating tabernacles or edifices— temples and churches. As here suggested, these Episcopes or priests were invested with the prerogative of deciding who, from their acceptable conduct through life, deserved to be decently consigned to the tomb, when that conduct was measured by, and conformed to, a standard which the priests themselves had instituted. And observing that this moral discrimination with respect to the election of subjects for decent interment, exerted a powerful influence upon the morals and conduct of the people, it hence at once suggested to their minds the thought of carrying

the principle or overt policy a step further,
promising the credulous populace not only an
honorable disposal of their bodily remains after
death, but unending felicity in the world to come
(as a reward for well-doing), which country
lay beyond the river Styx. And thus this river
became the highway, or "the strait and narrow
way" to paradise beyond the grave. The grave-
yard, or cemetery, through which they passed,
and in which the bodies were deposited, was called
the Elysian fields, which was regarded as a place
of blissful sojournment, to be occupied transiently,
preparatory to their entrance into the abodes of
superlative felicity; while Tartarus, beyond the
river Acheron, was the place of consignment for
the wicked or those who were not faithful in
complying with the requisitions of the priests.
The entrance to this *post mortem* prison
(Tartarus) was guarded by the mastiff Cerebus
(a dog with a hundred heads). Into this
Tartarus the priests warned the credulous,
ignorant and superstitious populace they must
be thrust as a penalty for any delinquency or
neglect of duty they might be guilty of—not to
be punished eternally however, for endless
punishment was not yet invented or thought of.
They were only to be consigned to this fiery
underground prison for a period proportionate
to their crimes. And this fact was elaborated into

fiction, and thus originated the doctrine of future punishment in Egypt; and out of this grew the doctrine of endless punishment or "eternal damnation," as the priests lengthened the period of punishment from time to time as the public utility or their own cause and craft seemed to suggest the necessity for it, until it was finally made to reach to all eternity, and the culprit was told that he must "roll on a sea of fire," and kick, and flounder, and splash the melted brimstone during the endless ages of eternity. And thus we observe that:

A research into Oriental or ancient sacred history, reveals as an important fact, or, if you please, reduces the same to an important fact, that the natural apprehension or suspicion of all those philosophic minds, who, having long since investigated the nature of the priestcraft, set down the doctrine of future endless'punishment as the work of designing priests. Mythological history is exuberant with the evidence that the traditional scheme of punishment for human beings or human souls in another world for actions committed in this, was invented by the priesthood as one of their auxiliary means of promoting the interests of their craft. And, according to Grecian writers, the agents of Government, or administrators of law, joined with the priests, and likewise adopted the system as a more effectual manner of controlling the populace, and keeping them in subjection to the Government.

To state the thing in brief, priests and politicians "colleagued together," and invented the Devil and his domicile as scare-crows to frighten the ignorant superstitious masses into quiet, submissive allegiance to the ecclesiastical tribunals, namely, "the powers that be." That I do not misrepresent when I aver that the Devil and Hell-fire doctrines were concocted by designing priests and pettifoggers, to serve as bugbears to frighten their credulous and childish subjects into acquiescent submission to their assumed authority to prove it. We have some very ancient authority, to prove it. We have some ancient testimonies on this subject from Egypt, India and Greece. We will first call up Strabo, known as "The Geographer of Greece." He declares that:

"Plato (a Grecian priest) and the Brahmins, invented fables concerning the future punishments of Hell."

And he appears to justify the invention for he says:

"The multitude are restrained from vice by the punishments the gods are said to inflict upon offenders, and by those terrors and threatenings which certain dreadful words and monstrous forms imprint upon their minds. . . . These things the legislators used as scare-crows to terrify the childish multitude. They can not be governed by philosophical reasonings. They are not led by such means to piety, holiness and virtue, but this must be done by superstition, or the fear of the gods.

It is impossible to conduct women and the gross multitude, and to render them holy, pious and upright, by the precepts of reason and philosophy. The fiery torches and snakes of the furies and spears of the gods, and the whole ancient mythology are all fables employed as bugbears to overawe the credulous and simple" (Geo. Book). Mr. Robinson remarks on the above (see Hist. of India), that these ideas, afterward adopted in Europe, are precisely the same which the ancient Brahmins had adopted in India for the government of the great body of the people.

Polybius, the historian (born 200 years B.C.), declares in like manner:

"Since the multitude is ever fickle, full of lawless desires, irrational passions and violence, there is no other way to keep them in order but by the fear of the invisible world—on which account our ancestors, it seems to me, acted wisely when they contrived to bring into popular belief the notions of the gods, and of the infernal regions.

"Hell is useless to sages, but necessary to the blind and brutal populace."

So the whole secret is out, that the soul-roasting doctrine of the ancient Pagans, copied into the Christian Scriptures, and transmitted through Christian credulity and superstition down to the present day, was not designed for sensible and intelligent people, but to frighten fools with. And those good Christians, who in this enlightened day and age of the world, still hold to this ancient superstition or myth, should not 'complain if we rank them with this class, seeing that it is historically demonstrated that no other class of people were expected to believe it but fools.   For this is the testimony not of one or two writers only, but of all who wrote on the subject thousands of years ago in Egypt, India and Greece, and they were many. They all concur with Strabo and Polybius in representing the doctrines of Devils, and *post mortem* punishment, as having been fabricated for the special benefit of the low, ignorant and superstitious populace. If space would allow it, I might quote in proof from Cicero, Dyonisius, Seneca, Socrates, Virgil, Livy, Plutarch, and Zimæus. The last named writer (Zimæus or Timæus) says, in figurative illustration:

"For as we somtimes cure the body with unwholesome remedies, when such as are most wholesome produce no effect, so we restrain those minds with false relations which will not be

persuaded by the truth. There is, therefore, a
necessity for instilling the dread of those foreign
torments reserved to the criminals in Tartarus,
and also, by the other fictions, which Homer (900
B.C.) has found in the ancient sacred opinions.''

As Homer's time was several hundred years
before Christ, this declaration makes the doctrine
of future punishment of very ancient existence.
This poet, whom some chronologists place 900
B.C., is here represented as finding the doctrine
in the then "ancient sacred opinions."

I will quote but two other Roman and Grecian
writers, Seneca and Cicero. The former tells us
that:

"Those things made the infernal regions
terrible, the darkness, the prison, the river of
flaming fire, and the judgment seat, are all a
fable with which the poets amuse themselves, and
by them agitate us with vain fears."

Cicero ranks the doctrine of future punishment with "silly fables," and Plutarch places it
with "fabulous stories." I will quote from one
author relative to the prevalence of this superstition in India three thousand two hundred years
ago, to show how it was looked upon by the more
intelligent classes of society, even in that remote
age and country. Colonel Dow, in his "Disserta-
tion on India," says:

"The more learned Brahmins affirm that the

Hell which is mentioned in the Vedas was only intended as a bugbear to enforce upon their minds the duties of morality. For that Hell is no more than a consciousness of evil, and those bad consequences which invaribly follow wicked deeds.''

Very sensible thoughts indeed to issue from the minds of heathens more than three thousand two hundred years ago; for the Missionary, Rev. D. O. Allen, places the compilation of the Vedas at 1400 B.C., while other writers assign it a much earlier date.

I will close my historical citations by brief quotations from two Christian writers. The Rev. Mr. Pitrat, in his ''Pagan Origin of Papalists' Doctrines,'' says:

''Indeed, there is no sort of torment that was not invented by legislators, mystagogues, poets and philosophers, to frighten the people under the false assumption of making them better, but the truth is, it was rather to keep them down in subjection'' (p. 138).

The Rev. Mr. Thayer says:

''Of course, in order to secure obedience, they were obliged to invent divine punishments for disobedience of what they gravely asserted to be divine laws.''

It will be observed, then that we have the most positive evidence, the most demonstrative historical proof, to establish this three-fold proposition:

1. That the doctrine of future endless torment, the after-death penal retribution, was extensively preached and promulgated in the Pagan world long prior to the era of the inauguration of Christianity.

2. That it was invented or hatched up by designing priests and law-makers, as a "rawhead and bloody-bones," to frighten those who might be simple or silly enough to believe it into loyal submission to their aspiring power—that the credulous, ignorant and superstitious masses or classes of society might thus become the pliant tools, the stepping-stones to the selfish ambition of the demagogues of both Church and State.

3. The learned or intelligent classes of society never believed the doctrine, nor was it expected that they would, as it was not designed for them. And hence those who now subscribe to this doctrine as being a literal reality, although they may be called Christians, cannot in a strict sense be called sensible and intelligent people.

"He who hath ears to hear let him hear," and with reference to future punishment, banish all fears.

We deem it proper to remark here, that we have omitted a direct reference to the authorities for many of the historical facts exhibited in the preceding pages of this work, simply because we found it would burden the work, and swell it to an inconvenient size. But in proof of our most important statements, we have in most cases given the name and page of the author. If the reader, however, will consult the following works, with those already named, he will find nearly all the facts contained in this book, and many others of a similar character, viz: Baily, Dupins, Bryant, Faber, Taylor, Theon, Kirker, Staffer, Boyer, Scalinger, Seldon, Macrobius, Virgil, Nonnus, Hyde, Creden, Higgins, etc.

CHAPTER XVI

The word Hell is the genitive case of the Anglo-Saxon word *hole*, and was used with reference to the imaginary future home of the wicked, as being in a hole somewhere in the earth —perhaps "Symmes' Hole."

The word Tartarus is from Tartary, being first used with reference to an imaginary abyss supposed to be located in Independent Tartary, and was the fancied abode of the wicked after death. It was believed to be "a dreadfully cold place; and Hesiod speaks of it as being a "deep dark place."

The word *infernus* means *inferior, under, below,* and was used to designate the fiery world "under or below the earth." Hence comes infernal.

Gehenna, used twelve times in the Greek, and always translated Hell, is from the two Greek words *ge* or *gen,* "The earth," and Hinnom, the name of the place where "The Lord's Holy People" were in the habit of sacrificing doves, pigeons, etc., and sometimes their own children.

115

Hence, it simply means, "the land," or rather "The Valley of Hinnom."

Tophet is from *Toph*, a "drum" (see Jer. 7: 31), beaten during the sacrifice of children (by the Lord's chosen people" as we have already stated), in order to drown their cries and shrieks. It was afterwards used to designate a depository for the carcasses of dead animals and other filth. And from these circumstances it came to represent the imaginary place for the punishment and torment of the wicked.

The word *Hades* has been explained in a previous chapter.

CHAPTER XVII

There is both a logical view and a moral view
of the doctrine of future endless punishment
which we have not space to present here. We
will, therefore, conclude this essay on the
"Biography of Satan," with a series of brief
questions, designed in lieu of an elaborate dis-
quisition on these points, and covering the ground
to present a compendious and comprehensive view
of the whole subject of *post mortem* punishment:

1. Who created the Devil, and when, and also
what is now his age?

2. What is his type or race, Malay, Mongolian,
African or Caucasian?

3. Of what kinds of material was he originally
composed, constituted, or created?

4. Assuming that he was made of nothing
(the materials of which the whole universe was
created, according to Webster), must we not hence
conclude, that he is still, and must ever continue
to be, nothing, in view of the philosophical axiom,
that everything must possess the qualities of the
materials of which it was originally composed?

5. If, however, His Infernal Majesty was not created by God, are we not then compelled to set him down as self-created or self-existent?

6. And if so, does it not then follow that we have two omnipotent, omnipresent and Almighty Beings?

7. And if two, we would ask, how many Almighty and Infinite Beings can exist at a time?

8. Or can we admit the existence of more than one in any other sense than that implied in the Otaheitan tradition, that "a Devil or God can dwell within a God as a snake within a snake?"

9. Or if God was the first Omnipresent Being, and filled all space by what process was room found for another omnipresent being?

10. And here the correlative query arises, also, is the "Grand Adversary of Souls" dependent on, or is he independent of, God?

11. If dependent on God, are we not logically compelled to consider God responsible for all his wicked, nefarious and diabolical deeds?

12. But if independent of God, how will we dispose of the philosophical absurdity of two Infinite, Almighty and Omnipotent Beings holding at the same time the reins of universal government?

13. Or if his Satanship is not omnipotent, how does he manage to "decoy millions of souls

to endless ruin," when "God wills that all should be saved?"

14.   And if not self-existent does it not follow that God must have created him?

15.   And if God did thus bring into existence "the Great Prime Mover of Evil," then is not God himself the author of Evil, inasmuch as without a Devil (according to Orthodox showing), there could have been no evil?

16.   Who then is responsible for the existence of evil, God or the Devil?

17.   Or how can God hate evil and yet allow the Devil to exist, when he possesses omnipotent power, and hence is able to destroy him?

18.   And if the Devil is a "fallen angel," as Christians teach, who tempted him and caused him to fall?

19.   Or how could he be tempted, when as yet there was no "Wicked One" to tempt him?

20.   Or would God have created him if he had known that he would turn out to be so naughty, nefarious and diabolical?

21.   And if he did not know it, how could he be omniscient or be the All-Wise-God?

22.   And how could this primarily perfect archangel fall in heaven where everything is and *must* be perfect—*infallibly* perfect?

23.   And if (as we are notified in "Holy Writ") "it came to pass" once upon a time, there

was "war in Heaven," may not such bloody conflict occur again and consequently all Garrisonian non-resistants be compelled to leave, or have their feelings and principles outraged by the exhibition of carnage and blood, they being in principle opposed to wars and fighting?

24.   Or shall we conclude they will prefer not to enter such a blood-stained paradise, but in preference "travel the broad road that leads to destruction?"

25.   And what security have we that the next "war in Heaven" among "the spirits of the just *made perfect*," will not result in a victory in favor of "Old Nick" and his rebel host, and the Old Dragon thus to drag himself on to the Emerald throne, and bring all the Celestials under, and henceforth wield his demoniac power over the whole Heavenly host?

26.   Can anything exceed the injustice of allowing the Devil to "transform himself into an angel of light," seeing that it is impossible to distinguish him from a celestial being while in this character, and hence impossible to know when to "resist" him, as the Bible enjoins?

27.   Assuming that his Satanship had a beginning, may we ask what was the *modus operandi* employed to make known his infernal existence, whether it was by the current mode of making known important truths, that of divine revelation

by and through the Holy Ghost, or whether he drew up with his fiery steed at the bar of the world in *propia persona,* and thus announced his diabolical existence?

28.   Why is "Holy Writ" silent on this important matter?

29.   And when (may we be allowed to ask) was the Great Bottomless Pit first discovered or *brought to light?*

30.   And how was it brought to light?   Did it turn up on a voyage of discovery for a "Northwestern Passage," or "Polar Inlet?"

31.   And we would like to ask, by what right and title does His Infernal Majesty hold his fiery pit or brimstone dominions.   Does he possess it in *fee simple,* or by the right of "squatter sovereignty?"

32.   And do we not discover the strongest proof of the matchless skill and wisdom of the Divine Architect in constructing the demoniacal pit without a bottom, seeing that without such a wise arrangement it must long ere this have been full to overflowing?

33.   Though it may be asked, what in the absence of a bottom prevents the impish inmates from falling through?

34.   Whether they are hung on hooks, provided for the purpose, in the sides of the pit?

35.   Or whether, being fledged (as Milton tells

us) they are required to "keep on the wing?"

36.   And were not the Great Bottomless Pit minus a bottom (seeing that thousands are daily dropping into it according to Orthodox preaching, and have been for six thousand years), may we not suggest that those in the bottom must ere this have been totally smothered to death?

37.   And if (as Buffom calculates) two hundred persons die every minute, and one hundred and fifty of these are precipitated into Pandemonium, we would like to ask, how many Imps, Demons, or Demi-Devils, must be incessantly employed in carrying off the sinful, reprobate souls, and tumbling them overboard into Tartarus, their new fiery home, where there is to be "gnashing of teeth" (or gums if no teeth), forever and ever?

38.   Or if not carried, how are they conveyed or conducted into Hades?

39.   Do they ride, walk, crawl, fly or hop?

40.   And are they coaxed to go, hired, led, pulled, or dragged?

41.   And as the Bible speaks of the incumbent ruler of the nether kingdom in the singular number as Satan, "The Devil," etc., we would like to ask how one "Unwearied Adversary" can possibly attend to every son and daughter of Adam, amounting to 1,000,000,000 souls (as all are tempted, we are taught), in the way of decoying

them into endless perdition, if he is not omnipresent?

42. Would he not have to move in his "giddy rounds" with the celerity of the telegraph to make calls but once *per annum* upon each son and daughter of Adam—leaving him scarcely time as he hauls up to the humble domicile or gorgeous palace of each, to bow and scrape, with a "How do you do, sir?" "Glad to see you."

43. Or are we to assume, in order to dispose of this difficulty, that as "nothing is impossible with God," so nothing is impossible with the Devil?

44. Or if the difficulty is attempted to be surmounted by supposing and assuming that his Satanic honor is supplied with a numerous retinue of subaltern imps or pigmy demons (subordinate or second-class officers) to aid him in his maleficent enterprise, we ask whether he would not, in that case, have to engross all his time in drilling, training, and posting these auxiliary or subsidiary functionaries in their new vocation of soul-catching?

45. And whether this would leave him any time to eat and sleep, or even to rest upon the Sabbath?

46. We would likewise query, whether, in high latitudes or in northern climates (say the icy Polar regions), if any of the hobgoblin board

of soul-catching demons should venture out from their intensely caloric fiery dominions while the thermometer is perhaps ranging at 50 or 75 degrees below zero—stiffened limbs, a bad cold, and mayhap still more serious, if not fatal, consequences might not ensue?

47. And should we not calculate on the danger of some reprobate souls, foreordained to destruction, making their escape into paradise on these occasions of their demon pursuers being inevitably retarded in their operations by the weather?

48. Ought not God to be very thankful to old Harry Haulaway for taking the punishment of the wicked off his hands, since he has declared "the wicked shall not go unpunished," and hence would have to punish them himself if the Devil did not?

49. And since we learn that God has decreed that "the wicked shall be punished in Hell," and the Devil is his agent in performing the needful work, must we not therefore consider his Snakish Majesty as a truly faithful servant of the Lord, and a co-worker with him?

50. Or if the punishment of the wicked is to be set down as the Devil's doings exclusively, and yet God assents to it by permitting him to exist and achieve his hellish work, then he is not acting

in conformity with God's will, and hence performing his duty?

51. And does it not thence follow, also, that it is God, and not the Devil, who punishes the wicked—the latter being only an agent?

52. On the other hand, if we assume that God is really opposed to the Devil's operations and machinations, then does it not follow that his diabolical Majesty holds the supreme sway and compels God Almighty to hold a subordinate rank under him, and to be a kind of *secondary* Omnipotence?

53. And does not this follow from another assumption, viz: that the Devil's "broad road" into which so many "go in thereat," is much more thronged than the "narrow way that leadeth unto life?"

54. And may we not ask, if it was not labor lost to make "a house of many mansions," seeing so few tenants find their way to it, or are allowed to enter it?

55. May we not also consider the Christian "plan of salvation" a kind of lottery system or scheme, in which God and the Devil are the ticket holders—the wicked constituting the ballots?

56. And is it not the teachings of "Holy Writ" that his Infernal or Satanic Omnipotence drew Mother Eve as the first prize?

57. And since that "bit of good luck," has he

not drawn the major portion of the small fry—a much larger share than the Creator himself?

58. If the Devil, after the curtailment of his ubiquity or of his infinite power (as taught in Rev. vi:8), and after God had declared "All souls are mine," still managed to decoy most of them into his fiery domicile, how many souls do we suppose he would have left for God, if his power had not been curtailed?

59. If most "God's heritage" travel "the broad road which leadeth unto destruction," as "the Holy Scriptures" inform us then are we not to suppose there are "rooms to let" in "the house of many mansions?"

60. Is it not strange, that if the wicked are to be punished eternally in Hell, as declared (in Matt. xxv:46), that God should speak of the destruction of Hell in Hosea xii:14 (*i.e., sheol,* the Greek for Hell)?

61. How can the wicked be punished after they are destroyed, as taught in Matt. xxi:41?

62. Or how long can they continue to exist after being destroyed?

63. How can the souls of the wicked burn forever (see Matt xviii:8), without being consumed, since it is the nature of fire to reduce all combustible substances to ashes?

64. Would it not be a great acquisition in chemical art to find a substance that would thus

burn forever without being consumed, especially if it could be used for culinary purposes in countries where fuel is scarce?

65. Do we not make God a thousand times worse and more fiendish than the wickedest of his creatures when we talk of his punishing any being forever?

66. And do we not invest him with an inhuman, brutal and savage character, which the most blood-thirsty tyrant who ever drenched the earth in human blood, would spurn to own?

67. For where in all history can the name of a demon-hearted villain be found who would burn an enemy even a week, not to mention an eternity?

68. Then, which is the worst to believe, such a libel on the character of God, or to believe the writer mistaken who assigns him such a character, even though said writer may claim to be inspired?

69. Is not Leigh Hunt right, when he says: "If an angel were to tell me to believe in eternal punishment, I would not do it, for it would better become me to believe the angel a delusion than God monstrous, as we make him by considering him the author of eternal punishment?"

70. How could a Being who is perfectly good and kind-hearted, punish one of his creatures without mentally, if not physically, punishing himself and thus himself suffer eternal misery and torment by such an act?

71. And is it not the climax of absurdity thus to assume that God would or could punish himself in this manner?

72. Or could a God with one spark of sympathy, justice, or mercy, punish a being (especially one of his own children) a year, a month, or even a day, to say nothing of eternity?

73. Would there be any sense in punishing a being for any other purpose than to reform him, or make an example for others?

74. Would it not be impossible for *post mortem* punishment to serve either of these ends?

75. Could a just God punish one of his creatures for acting out the impulses of that nature which he himself had endowed him with, and does not every human being do this?

76. When God (according to the Bible) saw that the greater portion of mankind were going to destruction, and creation proved a failure, why did he not knock the whole thing into "pi," and try it over again, or give it up for a bad job?

77. Is it not strange, that an Almighty and Omnipotent God, who "wills that all men should be saved," could not hit on some plan by which all could be saved?

78. Did God foresee man's proclivity to damnation or destruction?

79. If not, how could he be omniscient, or a God at all?

80. But presuming that he did foresee it, and was unable to see this fatal tendency 'to ruin, should he not have refrained from bringing him into existence?

81. Must we not consider it a cruel act to bring him into existence under such circumstances?

82. Could any being possessing a spark of feeling or sensibility, whether he be God or man, be happy for a moment with the consciousness that one single soul was suffering the woeful torments of Hell?

83. Could any man ever smile if he really believed that he had a friend or relative suffering, or doomed to suffer, unending misery in a lake of fire?

84. Or could he avoid hating a God after knowing that he had consigned his wife or child to the excruciating agonies of unquenchable fire?

85. Or could a man consistently be a father while holding such a doctrine as this?

86. For how could any man of feeling or principle consent to bring children into existence with the liability and even probability of the greater portion of them being lost, as he must presume they will be if "few are saved," as the Bible teaches?

87. We might ask, how can God punish any soul eternally, when it is positively declared in

his "Word," "The Lord will not cast off forever" (Lam. iii: 31).

88. Can there be any justice or sense in punishing all men alike in the world of woe, when there is such a vast difference in the nature of crime—a world-wide difference there is, for example, between stealing a penny and killing a man?

89. Indeed, are we not warranted in concluding that it would be morally impossible for a God of justice to inflict infinite punishment upon a mere finite being for any crime whatever, as it would be impossible for eternal consequences to grow out of any finite action either good or bad, without overthrowing the last principle of moral equity and common justice, and even common sense?

90. And do we not make God egregiously inconsistent after he has commanded us to love our enemies, to represent him as punishing his eternally, especially as he can (according to Phil. iii: 21) "change their vile hearts at any time?"

91. In what sense can Jesus Christ be the "Savior of all men," as taught in Tim. iv: 10, when we are told that they are not all saved, but the greater portion lost?

92. And what good does a belief in Hell or future punishment do when nearly all the crime

committed in the world is perpetrated by believers in endless misery?

93. Indeed, does not the belief in a Devil or Hell rather furnish a license for crime, by putting the evil day of punishment so far off that the sinner can calculate on a hundred chances of dodging it?

94. Can a man, with any sense of truth, be said to be virtuous, who refrains from evil or crime merely from fear of the Devil or a Hell?

95. If so, may not a dog be said to be virtuous when he refrains from depredations among poultry, observing the threatening aspect of his master's cane suspended over his head?

96. May not the Christian's Devil be properly denominated the Orthodox Bull Dog or "Scarecrow General to the Kingdom Come," seeing that he is employed to drive or scare free agents into Heaven?

97. Can a man truly be said to be free in any sense when chased into Heaven as a refugee from an all-devouring enemy, or when he turns his face Heavenward because pursued by a fire-vindictive, ferocious Devil?

98. Being thus frightened into Paradise, can he receive the answer, "Well done?"

99. Must we not conclude that a Christian possesses pretty strong proclivities to damnation, seeing it requires two omnipotent powers to save

him—that of the All-loving and coaxing Father going before and saying "Come unto me all ye ends of the earth," and be saved; and that of the Devil-driving pressure of the "Unwearied Adversary," who pursues him day and night, roaring on his track like a lion?

100. Seeing, then, that notwithstanding two omnipotent powers are set to work upon the Christian to get him into Heaven (one in front and the other in the rear), yet but few reach the kingdom—but few are saved (the elect only), are we not hence to conclude that a Christian is pretty hard to save?

101. Especially, as he has two passports to Heaven, besides the fear of the Devil—one is the forgiveness of sins the other is the atonement which cancels them?

102. May we not reasonably conclude, that if God wished to punish his children, he could do it without the aid of fire, or Devils, or Serpents?

103. As we are told, the Serpent caused the sin of our first parents, must we not conclude his creation was a blunder, and that Omniscience would not have created him at all if he had known he would have turned out to be so diabolical and devilish, but rather have let him remain "without form and void," especially as he must have had but little of the raw material (of nothing) left to

make him of, after making so many worlds of this material?

104. And if the "ruin of the race" was caused (as we are told) by the Serpent presenting Mother Eve with an apple, we ask if he should not be pardoned, in view of the fact, that he must have been pretty much of a gentleman and pretty well brought up thus to offer the fruit to others, and the lady first of all, before helping himself?

105. And as this fruit was calculated to "make wise unto salvation," and the Serpent "became wiser than any beast of the field" (see Gen. iii: 1) must we not hence conclude he did ultimately help himself pretty freely to the luscious fruit?

106. And, as we are told, our primeval parents "got their eyes open" and came "to know good from evil" by eating the forbidden fruit (see Gen. iii: 22), may we not ask how long they would have had to "go it blind," had they not stolen some of the sacred and forbidden fruit?

107. And are we not compelled to conclude that it was a very necessary and a very righteous act of stealing and sinning, seeing that if they had not pilfered some of the tempting pippins, they would never have known good from evil?

108. Are we not therefore indebted to the "Father of lies" (his Serpentship), for the most important truth ever disclosed to mankind, that

of "the knowledge of good and evil," seeing that
he instigated the act which led to this knowledge?

109. If eating the forbidden fruit was calculated to make Adam and Eve "wise as the gods,"
"ye shall be as gods knowing good and evil,"
(Gen. iii: 5), would they not have been the veriest
fools to refuse to eat, especially as it was so
luscious and inviting to the taste?

110. Which told the truth, Moses' imaginary
God or the Devil, *alias* the Serpent, when the
former told Adam "In the day thou eatest there-
of thou shalt surely die" (Gen. ii: 14), while the
"Father of lies," or talking Serpent, declared,
"Ye shall not surely die" (Gen. iii: 4), seeing
that "Adam lived nine hundred and thirty years
and begat sons and daughters?"

111. Indeed, does not God (according to
Moses) himself most explicitly admit that his
lying Snakeship was right, and he (Omnipotence)
wrong when he announced to the trinity or family
of gods, "behold the man is become as one of us,
to know good and evil" (Gen. iii: 22)?

112. How then can the Serpent-Devil be
justly charged with deceiving our first parents,
when God himself thus admits he told them the
truth?

113. If the Serpent of Genesis is the Devil of
Christendom, the great prime central wheel of
Orthodoxy, the same which Brigham Young

declares is after sinners with a "sharp stick," to whip them into Heaven, and which he also declares makes more saints than all other means combined (the power of God not excepted), then why was nothing said about roasting or broiling our primitive parents in "the kingdom prepared for the Devil and his angels," for their high-handed infractions of the divine commands?

114. Could not the great and dire calamity and curse which befell the human race, through the malicious agency of a Serpent (according to Orthodoxy), have been easily and most effectually avoided by simply making the fence, which enclosed the golden garden, snakeproof, so as to keep his Long-tailed Majesty out, or else by placing the angel with the flaming sword at the gate before the fall of man instead of after, so as to "bruise his head" or decapitate him on his un-warrantable attempts to enter?

115. As the Serpent after the fall-curse was doomed to crawl ("upon thy belly shalt thou go," Gen. iii: 14) the question arises, how did he travel previous to the fall. On which did he walk, his head or his tail, or did he hop or fly?

116. Is the Christian bard right, who declares,

"God made the Devil, and the Devil made sin,
So God Almighty made a hole to put the Devil in?"

117. In order to become fully "wise unto

salvation," should we not be informed in what language the Serpent talked to Mother Eve? Was it a living or dead language?

118. Must we not suppose that Mother Eve was surprised to hear a serpent talk, or shall we conclude she was familiar with such oddities?

119. Did the Serpent, otherwise Satan (for proof they are both one, see Rev. xii), furnish the first instance of walking without feet or legs, or had the curse expired and his legs grown out when he came from "walking to and fro in the earth," to pay his respects to old Job, and honor him with a visit?

120. How could it be a curse upon the Serpent to be doomed to crawl, when serpents and lizards that now crawl fare as well as toads that hop, or animals that walk?

121. Or is it more of a curse for snakes or serpents to crawl than the hundreds of other species of reptiles which travel in this way?

122. If the Serpent-Devil lost all his legs by an act of pure kindness in handing around the pippins instead of ill-manneredly monopolizing them all himself, had he not some cause to complain for being rendered legless, and may this not be the reason he is now "the Grand Adversary" of Moses' God?

123. What headway could the Serpent have made eating dust ("Dust thou shalt eat all the

days of thy life'' Gen. iii: 14)? Must it not have been a pretty tedious operation with his long-forked, spindle-shanked tongue, and did he grow lean or fat on such nutriment, and was mud, we may ask, a substitute for dust in wet weather?

124. Was the Devil a free agent before the fall or crawl? If not, how could he be the subject of a curse?

125. Is it true that there is now more enmity between the seed of the woman and the Serpent (see Gen. iii: 15) than at present exists between mankind and hyenas, rats and polecats?

126. How much enmity exists between the Hindoo juggler and his snake which entwines around his neck and crawls through his bosom?

127. As father Adam was doomed to eat the ground, ''cursed is the ground for thy sake, in sorrow shalt thou eat of it all the days of thy life'' (Gen. iii: 10), we ask if man had not become mortal, and short-lived by the curse, but all his future progency had continued to live here for-ever, how long would it have been before the race would have multiplied to a suffecent extent to have eaten up all the ground, consumed the whole earth, and left not a molehill to stand upon?

128. Which may we suppose ate the most ground or dust, father Adam or the Snake?

129. And why does not man continue to eat the ground now?

130.   May we not conclude that it is because he got his eyes opened by the curse, that he now possesses too much sense and intelligence to eat the ground, "as the Lord said unto Moses?"

131.   As we are told that the Devil on a certain occasion set Christ on a pinnacle of the temple, may we be allowed to be so curious as to inquire how the operation was performed—whether he was carried like Habakuk by the hair of his head, and whether he made any resistance to the operation?

132.   Must we not conclude that the Devil was a pretty able lawyer, from the skill and knowledge which he displayed in his arguments with Christ?

133.   And also well read in the Bible, as he quoted Scripture quite flippantly?

134.   And is it not rather dishonorable to the character of an · omnipotent and omnipresent God to represent him (as Christ is represented) as following Satan about like a haltered sheep or an old associate?

135.   Were the Evangelists, who relate so many cases of Christ casting out devils, aware that it was an old heathen superstition of various countries?

136.   When the devils entered the swine on Christ's permission as related (Luke viii: 32), which end, stem or stern, served as "the porch of entry" (as Erin expresses the idea)?

137. And had the hogs been sold while the devils were ensconsed in their "inner man," what discount should have been made to the buyer for tare (tear) so as to come at the net weight?

138. And should such diabolical occurrence take place now-a-days, would it not render the pork speculation rather a precarious business?

139. How high above this globular earth must Jesus and the Devil have been elevated to enable him to see "all the kingdoms of this world," including those on the under side?

140. Why is it that superstition could always find a devil anywhere, while science could find him nowhere?

141. And why is it that in countries where there are no priests, Devils are and ever have been as scarce as June-bugs in December?

142. Does not this circumstance demonstrate that the priest and the Devil are a kind of Siamese twins, inseparably connected and each indispensable to the other?

143. And is not the cause of this intimate relationship disclosed by the fact, that the Devil superstition tends to keep the wheels of priest-craft in motion, furnishes the oil, greases the gudgeons, and more than all, keeps the priest's pockets replenished with "filthy lucre?"

144. Is it not a historical fact, that Strabo, Polybius, Zimmæus, and various other Pagan

writers, who lived long before Christ, spoke of a
Devil and a Hell as being the invention of priests
and law-makers, concocted wholly and solely for
the purpose of scaring the credulous, ignorant and
superstitious populace into obsequious subjection
to "the powers that be"—*i.e.*, priests and
potentates?

145. And why does not the Christian Bible
revelations reveal the important fact, that its
Devil and hell-fire doctrines are those of Pagan
origin, and mere heathen superstition?

146. As then, the ancient Pagan philosophers
show, that the notion of a Devil and a Hell were
fabricated to frighten fools with, does it not thence
follow that all who now believe in this superstition
should be ranked in this class?

147. Which is the most merciful and reasonable being, the Christian's God which they tell
us punishes to all eternity, or the heathen Devil
of Siam, which only punishes a thousand years,
according to the Siamese?

148. And must we not consider the Persian's
God, too, as more reasonable and merciful than the
Christian's God, inasmuch as he promises to let
"Old Splitfoot," or Plug Ugly himself, ascend
from Limbo to Paradise in the course of fourteen
thousand years and his whole rebel host with him?

149. And which should we consider the best
and most reasonable being, the Bible God, who

told Abraham to murder his son Isaac, or the
Devil who told him not to do it?

150.   Is it not strange that men can ascribe to
God a character which they know angels would
spurn, and they themselves would blush to own?

151.   Has not the principal effect of preaching
the Hell-fire superstition been to make numerous
Hells on earth, without saving any from an
imaginary Hell hereafter, as it has made
thousands miserable with foolish fears?

152.   And has not the practice of representing
God as damning a portion of the race had the
evil effect also of causing men to damn each other,
and is thus the principal source—the primary
fountain—of all profane swearing with which all
Christendom is now cursed and demoralized from
one end to the other?

153.   Is it not true that from "God damn
you," in the Bible and the pulpit, comes the "God
damn you" heard from a thousand lips daily in
the streets?

154.   Is it not true, also, that the doctrine of
endless punishment is only calculated to operate
upon the "weak spots" of the weakest people—in
other words, the weakest portion of their natures,
and thus is only a bugbear for weak-minded
grown-up children?

155.   Why is not the Devil now frequently seen
and encountered as in the days of Martin Luther,

who threw his inkstand at his "devoted head," and who seriously relates several disputes and combats he had with him; and many professed to see him daily?

156. Is it not because his Snakish honor is afraid of the daylight of science and infidelity?

157. And may we not reasonably calculate, that the "march of science and infidelity" will soon drive him and his demon host back into the dark ramparts of superstition, for another thousand years?

158. And may we not assume that society will prosper as well morally without a Devil, after his Majesty has given up the ghost, the priesthood only excepted?

159. And is not the Scriptural fact, that neither Paul nor John make any mention of a Hell, some evidence that it is not an indispensible institution?

160. Or, if it were, should we not be informed which Hell sinners are put into first—the fiery Hell spoken of in Matt. v: 22, or the Hell of "outer darkness" (see Matt. viii: 12), where there is to be "wailing and gnashing of teeth?"

161. In conclusion, we would ask, if there were a Hell, whether it is not probable that some ingenious Yankee imp would soon construct an underground railroad and run off or let out all the fiery prisoners?

162. Or may we not reasonably conjecture that the angels in Heaven, while bending over the battlements of Paradise, and gazing into the awful pit below, would be moved to shed tears enough to put out the fires of Hell, and thus permit the subjects of perdition to ascend to the regions of heavenly bliss?

163. And finally, as several of the Christian sects have, since the dawn of science and civilization, cast the Devil out of their Bibles (*i.e.,* deny his being recognized there) may we not reasonably hope that the time is not far distant when all sensible men can stand alone in the path of moral rectitude without the aid of such old, obsolete baby-jumpers to frighten them into piety and Paradise, as the Devil and Hell-fire superstitions are?

The foregoing queries are not intended to cast ridicule on the Christian Bible, or any of its believers, but simply to present the absurdities of the doctrine of future endless punishment in its true and strongest light.

APPENDIX

"And there was war in Heaven: Michael and his angels fought against the Dragon, and the Dragon fought and his angels" (Rev. xii: 7).

There is scarcely an Oriental nation whose religion has been commemorated in history, but that has preserved in its traditions the story of a celestial battle or "war in Heaven," similar to that referred to in the above text. Titan, according to the Roman legends, rebelled against Jupiter, and thereby stirred up a war in Heaven. But Jupiter prevailed and cast him and his rebel host over the battlements of Heaven (as Michael and his angels did the Dragon), and imprisoned them under mountains, where they

"From our sacred Hill (Holy Mountain) with fury thrown,
Deep in the dark Tartarian gulf shall ever groan."

And it was the belief of the superstitious classes that it was the attempt of this infernal host to rise and liberate themselves which produced all the earthquakes and volcanoes. And the battle of the Titans (children of Heaven) against the gods of Olympus in the other world, is found in mythological traditions of ancient Greece. And then we have in Egyptian traditions the story of

Typhon (the Devil) rebelling and making war against Oshiret or Osyrus, who cut him to pieces. The Chinese relate a battle between the inhabitants of the clouds and the stars—the Lamb (''the Lamb of God that taketh away the sins of the world''), headed the starry host and conquered. With the Persians, who seem to have the original copy or edition of the story, the scene was an astronomical one. A war broke out between the summer God and winter God, which was simply a contest between the seasons of summer and winter—that is, between heat and cold. The winter God was hurled out of Paradise and became a fallen angel. Each had a retinue of subordinate angels, as in St. John's case. And here we will call attention to a curious circumstance in the choice of names which St. John selected for the principal combatants in his account of the celestial combat. Michael is his good angel, and Dragon his bad or wicked angel. Now let it be noted here, that the last syllable of Michael is *el*, which is the Hebrew name for God (the genitive case being Eloi), *''Eloi lama sabacthani''* is a prayer to God in the Hebrew language. And *On*, the last syllable for Dragon, is the Egyptian name for God. Hence, it is simply the Hebrew God *El* in battle array against the Egyptian God *On*. And of course St. John would represent that the Hebrew God or angel

God, Michael, conquered. *On* was also a name for God among the Babylonians. And it is a curious circumstance, that whenever the Hebrew and the Hebrew-descended Christians (hating as they did the Egyptians and Babylonians, because they had conquered and enslaved their ancestors), had occasion to refer to or speak of the God of either of these nations, they would employ some odious even devilish title as the Drag-on, Typh-on, Dag-on, Abad-on, Appolly-on, Pyth-on. Some of these were very honorable, lofty and sacred titles or names for God among the ancient Babylonians and Egyptians. But the Jews and Christians have dragged down their Gods and converted them into Devils; or rather, they have stolen their sacred title for God, and rendered it odious by applying it to the Devil; as Typh-on, Dag-on, The Drag-on, etc. While, on the other hand, they defied some of their own angels and ancient worthies by attaching to their names, either at the commencement or termination, the Hebrew title for God-*el*, as Gabri-el, Isra-el, El-isha, El-ijah, etc. They were thus God-ified or deified. In view of these facts, it is not to be wondered at that St. John should speak of Babylon (Babyl-on) as being "the mother of harlots and abomination" (Rev. xvi: 5), and rank Egypt with Sodom (Sod-om, on and om being the same) and Gomorah; and the Bible

writers should use the name of both Egypt and
Babylon as synonymous for everything hateful,
disdainful, odious, or wicked. It was but the
natural, practical or wicked out-working of their
pent-up feelings of revenge. And thus the great
enigma of the "Mystery of Babylon" is solved.

Reader, please reflect upon these things.

ANGELS FALLING AND BECOMING THEREBY CONVERTED INTO DEVILS AND DRAGONS

The belief has obtained wide acceptance in the
Christian world, that the Devil *alias* the Dragon,
is "a fallen angel." And St. John speaks of the
Dragon falling (from his angelship) and being
cast into the bottomless pit (see Rev. xx: 1). And
how did old Captain Dragon (Captain of the
infernal goats) fall, let us enquire? Why, he
simply fell into the hands of Christendom who
assumed the license to metamorphose him from a
God to a Devil. They Drag-ed him from the
throne of God in the Babylonian and Egyptian
heavens, armed with horns, hoofs, and tail, and
converted him into a Devil—a fallen angel,
Dragon, and cast him into the "bottomless pit,"
in retaliation for the bondage endured at
the hands of these nations in times past. And as
this Dragon came down from Heaven, according
to the Mystic and Apocalyptic St. John, his tail
becoming entangled among the starry worlds, tore

one-third of them loose from their orbits and precipitated them down upon our little planet. (We suggest that he must have been nearly all *tail*, or rather that the story is all a *tale*). No wonder that the "kingdom of Heaven suffered violence" (see Rev.). However, astronomically speaking, it is literally true; for according to Burritt's "Geography of the Heavens," the astronomical Dragon spreads over a large portion of the canopy, embracing at least five large constellations. And as to his falling, it is even so, for the Dragon (now the sign for October) under the name of *Scorpio*, has fallen. Being once away up in the harvest month (August) by the procession of the equinoxes, he fell lower and lower, until he sunk clear below the southern horizon into the "bottomless pit," or pit of darkness. The conception of "fallen angels" is neither new nor orignal to the Christian Bible. The Hindoo Bible, at least three thousand years old (the Vedas), gives in its third chapter a somewhat detailed account of the fall of angels, while the fourth chapter describes their mode of punishment, which consisted in being hurled down from their lofty positions in Paradise (because they rebelled against Heaven (*i.e.,* "the trinity in unity," Brahma, Vishnu and Diva) and were precipitated into Ondera, ("the deep, dark pit"), there to remain until "the Intercessor," called, also, "The Lamb of God," the second person in the Trinity, would plead for them and have them delivered; having first, however, to serve out their "thousand years' probation," which reminds us of St. John's Dragon being "bound for a thousand years" (see Rev. xii: 2). The Persian tradition of fallen angels found in their Bible (the Zend-Avesta), is somewhat similar excepting that out of thirty different orders of angels, they had but one to fall, who thereby became a "Peris"—a Devil.

INDEX

CPSIA information can be obtained
at www.ICGtesting.com
Printed in the USA
BVHW070539010219
539209BV00002B/207/P

9 781885 395115